POKER NATION

POKER
NATION

A HIGH-STAKES, LOW-LIFE ADVENTURE INTO THE HEART OF A GAMBLING COUNTRY

Andy Bellin

HarperCollins*Publishers*

HarperCollins books may be purchased for educational, business, or sales promotional use. For information, please write: Special Markets Department, HarperCollins Publishers Inc., 10 East 53rd Street, New York, NY 10022.

FIRST EDITION

Designed by Elliott Beard

Printed on acid-free paper

Library of Congress Cataloging-in-Publication Data

Bellin, Andy.
    Poker nation : a high stakes, low-life adventure /
by Andy Bellin.—1st ed.
      p.   cm.
Includes bibliographical references.
ISBN 0-06-019903-2
1. Poker. I. Title.
GV1251 .B45 2001
795.41'2—dc21   2001042409

02 03 04 05 06 ❖/RRD 10 9 8 7 6 5 4 3 2 1

For my brother Marco, who has inspired me all of my life

The guy who invented gambling was bright,
but the guy who invented chips was a genius.

—BIG JULIE,
a New York City gambler

There are few things that are so unpardonably
neglected in our country as poker . . . it is enough to
make one ashamed of one's species.

—MARK TWAIN

CONTENTS

ACKNOWLEDGMENTS

There are so many people who have helped me along the way that it's almost embarrassing. For brevity's sake I'll only do the greatest hits. Chronologically, my oldest debts are owed to George Plimpton and Jennifer Rudolph Walsh. Without either of their support, friendship, and heroic efforts on my behalf, I would have never published a single word.

This book came from an article that ran in *Esquire*. Without the opportunity afforded me by editors Scott Omelianuk and Mark Warren, this project would have never started. Which brings me to my close friend Ken Kurson. He has done more to further my career than anybody on the planet. If not for his encouragement and advice, I would have never signed with my agent, Becky Kurson, his wife. She was the perfect person to represent this book. Her patience and wisdom are the only reason that I'm not sitting here thanking a team of psychotherapists.

My father, Howard, and friends Steve Clark and David "Catbird" Hirshey all provided me with healthy advice during the writing of this. The greatest help during this saga has been, without a doubt, my girlfriend, Tessa Benson. She must have read every word of this thing twenty times. Thank you, Tessa.

My deepest debt is owed to my editor, Marjorie Braman. I don't know what kind of courage or insanity it takes to be willing to work with a first-time author as confused and clueless as me, but thank God she had it. She knew exactly what to say and when to say it. Her confidence in me meant more than anything during this very strange year. There's no way this book gets written with any other editor.

I cannot imagine a more fortunate experience than the one I had with HarperCollins. Every person I worked with was inspiring, patient, decent, and incredibly talented. Thank you all so much. Who knows, maybe I just finally got lucky.

(I include the following for the benefit of a number of friends whom I am too kind to mention by name.)

THE RANK OF HANDS—FROM LOWEST TO HIGHEST—IN POKER

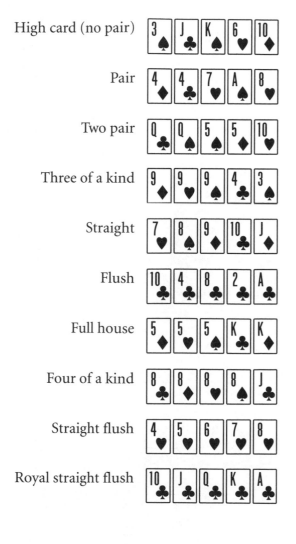

High card (no pair)	3♠ J♣ K♠ 6♥ 10♦
Pair	4♦ 4♣ 7♥ A♠ 8♥
Two pair	Q♣ Q♠ 5♠ 5♦ 10♥
Three of a kind	9♦ 9♥ 9♣ 4♣ 3♠
Straight	7♥ 8♠ 9♦ 10♣ J♦
Flush	10♣ 4♣ 8♣ 2♣ A♣
Full house	5♦ 5♥ 5♠ K♣ K♦
Four of a kind	8♣ 8♦ 8♥ 8♠ J♣
Straight flush	4♥ 5♥ 6♥ 7♥ 8♥
Royal straight flush	10♣ J♣ Q♣ K♣ A♣

IT'S MY DEAL

*If you look around the table and you can't tell who
the sucker is, it's you.*

—PAUL SCOFIELD,
playing the role of Mark Van Doren in *Quiz Show*

I am an excellent poker player. If I had to be more specific, my guess would be that I'm in the top .01 percentile in the world. That's a fancy statistic if you're talking about SATs or something like archery, but when it comes to poker, it can create an enormous problem. With somewhere in the neighborhood of 135 million people across the planet who play the game, a little eighth-grade math will tell you that there are about 135,000 people shuffling cards at this very moment who are better than me.

A bigger problem is that three or four of those individuals are usually seated at my card table on any given night. My home club, the Winchester—where I have spent around three thousand hours playing over the past three years—is in the heart of New

York City, where poker is technically illegal. That's kind of a sexy fact if you are one of those people who likes life a little dirty (which I do), but it also means that every individual in my club is the genuine article. There is no tourist/insurance salesman who just got lucky at the craps table wandering into my game like in Vegas or Atlantic City. We've got no sheep who bet into your flush with a straight thinking their hand is the winner.

At those casino tables, I'm a huge favorite to win. Almost any semiconscious human being is. An average casino game of Texas Hold'em poker is played with nine or ten people. If you're in a $500 buy-in game, and you've got two sheep at the table, that's $1,000 for the other six or seven of us to chop up. I just made 22 percent on my money, and I haven't even started to play. God bless America. But that's why my home club is so tough—no sheep.

So why play there? There was a big-time Wild West gambler named "Canada Bill" Jones. Asked once why he voluntarily played in a small-town game he knew to be crooked, Bill replied, "Because it's the only game in town." There's your answer.

The club is basically a low-rent glorified basement. On any given night you can find a hundred strippers, chiropractors, tax attorneys, and cabdrivers huddled around fifteen tables, stacking chips, shuffling cards, and watching sports. Some people even find time to eat their dinner there. That's the worst part—grown men shoveling forkfuls of food into their mouths at a panicked pace, trying not to miss a hand. Three burritos in four minutes can't be good for the digestion.

A typical night at my club is unlike a typical night anywhere else. These people are true originals. As the old adage goes: The only thing stranger than a poker player is the person sitting next to him.

"Jesus Christ, Morty! Deal the cards." Amy has no patience at a poker table. She is a beautiful, petite Filipino woman in her early forties who has a metabolism that could power the Vegas strip for two weeks straight. She's always moving, always doing something, talking, smoking, shuffling, and when she does sit still, she has a look in her eyes like she's going to combust at any moment. "Deal, or I'll cut your balls off!" Like I said, she's got no patience.

Morty, on the other hand, has all the time in the world. Slow by nature, he goes through moments of total disorientation and detachment, as if the minute dust particle floating by his face has taken complete control of his consciousness. These episodes could last forever if it were not for the caring attention his fellow cardplayers give to him. From under the table comes a noise that sounds suspiciously like a switchblade knife opening. Amy leans toward Morty, her hands out of sight, and says very slowly and deliberately into his ear, "Get the cards in the air, old man." Morty's back from the ethereal plane now. He deals.

Everybody thinks Morty—a garmento from Manhattan's Lower East Side in his late fifties—is losing his mind. In poker, when you "put" somebody on a hand, that means you're making an assumption about what they are holding. "I put that guy on two pair" means that's what you think he's got. Most people at the club put Morty on the early stages of Alzheimer's.

But I know what's really going on with him. Covered head to toe in silver American Indian jewelry, always well tanned from a week in Jamaica, Morty should be bronzed in the Natural History Museum as the last living semi-functional hippie. My read . . . I put him on burnout. When that tiny dust particle carries him off into his private little world, he's not trying to remember his girlfriend's name, or where he was born; he's back at Woodstock contemplating whether one or two hits of LSD is necessary to get him off just right for the upcoming Santana set. And remember this: Morty is a good cardplayer. He wouldn't be at the club if he wasn't. So most of the time, when he's daydreaming, he's doing it to piss everybody else off. Poker players play much worse when they're pissed. It's called being "on tilt." And Morty can tilt anybody. That's his gift.

He finally gets the cards in the air. We're playing no-limit Texas Hold'em. It's the perfect gambling game. Each player (there can be up to ten at a time) is dealt two cards down, called pocket cards. On the strength of these alone, the participants have to decide whether or not to play in that hand. Then five community cards are placed in the center of the table. They are shared by everybody. And from those seven cards (your two pocket cards plus the five on the board) each player makes his best five-card hand. The up cards are revealed in the following pattern: the first three at once (known as the flop), then the fourth alone (called the turn card), and then the last (the river card). There are betting opportunities between each round.

Most poker games have designed betting structures. A regular home game will usually have a maximum bet and a ceiling on the number of raises allowed (e.g. $3 max bet, with three raises). Casino games operate under similar rules, but they will usually have two levels of betting. In a $10–$20 game of Hold'em, those are the only amounts you are allowed to wager. The first two rounds of betting will be in the smaller denomination, and the last two will be in the larger. It doesn't allow for much in the way of creativity.

Some people find that regimented betting structure stifling, and prefer to play a version of the game without betting restrictions—no-limit. It grants total betting freedom. No guides, no restraints; you like your cards, you're welcome to bet every penny in front of you on them at any time. You can go from hero to zero in one hand. People say that limit Hold'em is a science, while no-limit is a true art.

In a game of Texas Hold'em, so many of the cards are shared by all the players that the winning hand is often decided by the narrowest margin. For example, if one player holds K♠ J♦ as his pocket cards, while another plays K♥ 10♣, and the board ends up looking like K♣ 4♠ 4♣ 9♦ 7♥, then the best hand the winner can make from his seven cards is two pairs—kings and 4s—with a jack as his fifth card (known as a kicker). The loser also makes kings and 4s, except his kicker would be a 10. Almost identical hands, the only difference being the smallest difference in the kicker, and that costs the loser the pot.

The use of community cards and the lack of betting restrictions is why no-limit Hold'em is considered the ultimate poker game. Therefore, it's the only game played in the main event of the World Series of Poker. Legendary gambler Johnny Moss once said, "Chess is to checkers what Hold'em is to draw or stud." It is that elaborate.

Hold'em is known in some circles as seven-card crack, and for good reason. Taking about two minutes to finish a game, hands come rapid-fire, one after another, endlessly providing players with an immediate way to recoup their losses or double up their winnings. And in Hold'em, unlike stud, there's no need to memorize the board or what cards got burned. That's the beauty: every hand is right in front of you to see, and since the primary components of the hand—the five up cards on the table—are shared by everybody, the rank of the winning hand will always vary. If there are not three of one suit on the board, there is no way to make a five-card flush. If there is no pair faceup, then a full house or four of a kind ("quads") are impossible. That's why the game is so seductive. Every time the cards are dealt, the best hand ("the nuts") always changes.

Like any other esoteric subculture, the world of poker has its own lexicon. Most of the time no one seems to be able to track the origin of the terminology we use. Some colloquialisms are obvious; a San Francisco Busboy describes a starting hand in Texas Hold'em of a queen and a 3. A queen with a trey . . . get it? A San Francisco Busboy, obviously. Other terms are more obscure, almost historic even. On August 2, 1876, a cattle herder named Jack McCall walked into a saloon in Deadwood, a small town in the Dakota territory, and shot the legendary Wild Bill Hickok in the back of the head. Hickok died instantly. His body fell forward, still holding his poker hand of two pairs—aces and 8s—which has been known as the Dead Man's Hand ever since. I have no idea where "the nuts" came from.

Figuring out the best possible hand in any given game is pretty easy. If the board looks like 2♣ 4♦ 8♠ 9♥ 10♣, then the nuts is a queen-high straight (having a jack-queen as your pocket cards). But with community cards like A♠ K♠ K♦ Q♠ Q♦, there is one way to make a straight, nine different kinds of flushes, five different possible ranks of full houses, and even two different ways to make quads. And that's not even the nuts. You'd only have the highest hand possible if you held the J♠ 10♠, making a royal straight flush. The power of any hand is totally dependent on what the nuts are for that specific game.

With Morty's deal complete, the game can finally get under way. We're playing shorthanded at the moment, which means that at a table meant for ten players, we've only got six. This changes the game some. With fewer participants, the value of lesser hands increases. At a short table you can play more hands, play them more aggressively, and bluff your way to more wins. I much prefer a shorthanded game, as it allows for more creativity. At this table, I'm sort of in the upper middle class in the poker hierarchy. One person is definitely better than me, two are about the same, and two are a little worse. This means if I play my "A game" and get decent cards, I should go home with about an extra grand in my pocket.

The heavyweight at the table is Wilson Terry, a forty-three-year-old bond trader from Guyana. He spends six nights a week at the card house. This could cause a problem in some marriages, but not his, because his wife is always at the table too. Wilson's game is sublime, almost artistic. His eyes are constantly flipping between the cards and the people at the table. He does this because most players have a "tell," some subconscious twitch or unnatural move that gives away what cards they are holding. And there are a million of them.

I had a tell when I first started playing regularly in graduate school. When I'd bluff or call somebody when my hand wasn't so strong, I'd subconsciously use small denominations to bet with.

I'd make a $10 wager using five $2 chips. I would only reach for the $10 marker when I had a huge hand. Even though that game was filled with burnouts and dope fiends, it didn't take them long to figure out when I was bluffing or when I had the nuts. A few months after I left graduate school (please note that I said "left grad school," not "graduated"), somebody from that game sent me an anonymous letter informing me of my twitch. I guess that guy liked me enough to want to save me from a lifetime of giving away my hand, but not enough to have told me while we were still playing together and take money out of his own pocket. Wilson Terry knows every tell in the book.

Dr. Liam Kelly is one of the guys at the table with skills on par with mine. A New York shrink born in Ireland, Liam has read more about poker than any person alive. He loves the game. Loves to play it, talk about it, think about it. He told me that he dreams more about poker than he does about sex. I always imagine some patient of his lying on his couch, bawling about their busted marriage, and Liam saying something like, "Yeah, yeah, cry me a river, I had pocket aces snapped three times last night." The word is that he's a great shrink, and he plays like it. Liam is what card players refer to as a rock . . . somebody who plays flawlessly, by the book, always making the proper decision. His only problem is that he hates losing. I mean really hates it. After a bad beat he gets all steamed up and tilts easily. That's what brings him down to my skill level.

I've just been dealt my down cards: 3♣ 3♠ (a pair of 3s, for some reason, are called crabs). Not a great hand, but because the table is so short, I decide to play aggressively. I raise $30. Liam takes a break from eating his dinner to check his cards and then matches my bet. Wilson's dealing; he's the only other caller.

The flop comes: J♣ J♥ 6♠ . This gives me two pair, jacks and 3s, but it's really not the best flop for my crabs, so I check. Liam looks at his cards again and then bets $50. Wilson folds, and I do the same. As Dr. Liam is sweeping in the chips, Wilson decides to show the hand he just folded: J♦ 10♦ . His two pocket cards, when combined with the flop cards, gave him three jacks. A very big hand. Everybody at the table is shocked by his fold. "Man, you flopped trips, that's a tremendous fold," Dr. Liam says.

"Jesus, I would have bet my G-string on those cards," Amy adds.

Wilson nods, "Any man taking time off from eating a steak and then bets into me has got to have me beat. I put you on queen-jack." Dr. Liam thinks for a second-then exposes his cards: K♠ J♠ . He had trip jacks with a better kicker than Wilson. The only way Wilson could have won the hand is if the turn or river cards were one of the three remaining 10s in the deck, giving him a full house. Liam was about a seven-to-one favorite after the flop. Usually a great night is not decided by how many big pots you win, but how many you don't lose. Wilson just avoided a brutal beating. "I give lessons on Tuesdays," Wilson says, smiling. He always says that. I keep my pocket 3s to myself.

After about an hour Joey Millman joins our game. This is not a good development. Joey is a monster, one of the best players I have ever seen. It's like my cards are transparent to him. I think about leaving the game. I'm up about $100, but it's still early, and well, this is the only game in town.

Hands come and go with no real impact on my bankroll until I deal myself the 8♣ 9♣. It's not a premium hand, but since we are playing no-limit, medium-size suited connectors can pay off big if you hit your hand. As the dealer, I have a huge advantage because I get to see all the action before deciding whether or not to play. The betting starts to my left and continues clockwise until it gets to me. Sometimes position is everything, almost more important than your cards.

Four people match Morty's $20 bet. Having a lot of callers makes my hand more enticing because there is more money in the pot, so I decide to join the fun. The flop comes: 6♥ 7♣ K♣. This is an encouraging turn of events for me. I have four of the five clubs I need for a flush (known as a "toilet flush," if my fifth club doesn't show), and also four of the five cards I need for a straight.

Morty opens the betting with $30. Dr. Liam raises the bet to $100. Amy folds, and then Joey Millman thinks for a second and calls the $100 cold. Now I have to try to figure out what the hell is going on. The best thing anybody could have at the moment is three of a kind (a set). I'm pretty sure that no one has a set of kings because the betting was too light before the flop for somebody to have "cowboys" as their pocket cards. But still, somebody might have a set of 6s or 7s. It could be Morty, maybe Dr. Liam; Joe's cold call tells me that he's probably got a king with a nice kicker. If he was on a bigger flush draw than mine—if he were holding [A♣][4♣] let's say—he would have tried to end the hand right there with a huge raise. So I put him on the pair of kings and go about trying to figure out what the rest of the table is holding.

Dr. Liam is too tight to bet an incomplete hand like a flush draw so hard after the flop, so I've got to put him on a made hand like a pair of kings or a set. But even in the worst scenario, Dr. Liam having three 7s, let's say, with two cards to come, I still have two chances at fourteen cards that will make me a winner (those possible winning cards are called outs). Another club would give me a flush (although the 6 of clubs could give somebody a full house or quads, so I don't consider that card helpful). That's eight outs. And combining my 8 and 9 with the 6 and 7 on the flop, I also have an open-ended straight draw. So any 5 or 10 gives me a straight. That's an additional six cards that will make me a winner (I am not counting the 5 or 10 of clubs, as I have already included them in my flush calculations). Add that up, and you get fourteen outs. As long as the board doesn't pair, and nobody is on a larger flush draw than me, I've got to be the favorite. I think about making a huge raise, but since Liam, Joey, and Morty are all acting like they have strong hands, I could be in all sorts of trouble, so I just call. Morty decides that the $70 raise is too much for him and folds. Maybe he had an ace-10 or a small pocket pair—regardless, he's done.

The turn card is the 5 of diamonds making the board look like: [6♥][7♣][K♣][5♦] . Add my 8 and 9 to the 5, 6, 7, and you can see that I make my straight. Now I know there's a God. And beyond that, I know he loves me. I've got the highest hand possible, the nuts; I am unbeatable. The only thing I have to think about now is how to make the most money from this divine gift.

Liam chooses not to bet, and so does Joey. It seems strange to me to have both of them check after so much action, especially since the turn card seemed so innocuous. So I conclude that Liam is slow-playing his three of a kind, sandbagging, or setting a trap to induce a bet so he can raise me. I suspect that Joey smelled Dr. Liam's check-raise coming and therefore did not want to bet his hand for him. Thing is, I want Liam to check-raise, I've got the nuts. So I make a tiny little bet in the hopes it looks like I'm trying to steal the hand. I do my best to seem nervous as I throw fifty bucks into the pot. Liam just calls, and so does Joey. Nobody came over the top of my bet with a raise. In short, I got greedy and missed a huge opportunity to end the hand right there.

I deal the river card. It's the jack of clubs. The complete board looks like: 6♥ 7♣ K♣ 5♦ J♣ . That's a scare card for the whole table. With three clubs now showing, a flush looks very possible, and I've got one, just not ace-high. Also, before the river, for somebody to have two pair, they would have had to play some awkward hand like a king-6, which is very unlikely considering the early betting. Now that there is a jack on board, two pair becomes likely because king-jack is a very playable hand. This is important because before the river was dealt, a person with king-queen as their pocket cards was beating somebody who played king-jack. But now that king-jack just turned into two pair, king-queen looks a lot less sexy. Liam knows that, and that's why he shakes his head as he checks. If he had a set, he would have check-raised the turn, so now I know he's got king-queen.

Joey smiles and asks the only question I don't want to hear: "What do you have in front of you, Andy?"

I count down my stack. "About a grand," I say.

Joey looks at his chips. "I've got two kittens." He pushes all his chips into the pot. "Okay, I tap. Two thousand to you."

"Tap," of course, means he's betting everything.

Within two milliseconds of his completing his sentence, I can feel tiny beads of sweat forming all over my body. Three minutes ago I was the very picture of elegance—Bond at the baccarat table in Monte Carlo—and now, now I'm the sweaty guy on the subway you don't want to sit next to.

In the early days of poker, players could be bet out of a hand if a wager exceeded the amount of money they had on the table. If there was a $10,000 bet to them and the person only had $500, he would either have to fold, secure a loan at the table, or put up some collateral like his children's life insurance policy. But now we've evolved into gentleman gamblers. We play "table stakes," meaning that a player is only obliged to bet what he has on the table. It's called going all-in. So even though Joey bet two grand, I'm only liable for the $1,000 I have in front of me. If Dr. Liam were to call, since he had enough money to cover Joey's bet, he would have to call the whole $2,000 to stay in the hand. A "side pot" of $2,000 would be created (one grand of Joey's and one grand of Liam's) for them to compete for. That way, if I ended up with the best hand, I am only eligible to win the main pot. Joey and Liam would then show their cards, and the better hand between the two of them would win the side pot, regardless of what cards I had. It doesn't really matter either way, as that sum represents every penny I have.

So what the hell do I do now? The last card improved my hand in the sense that I went from a straight to a flush, but I no longer have the nuts. That's now ace–anything of clubs. Was Joey on the nut flush draw after all? Or did he just make two pair and thinks that's good enough to win? I can't tell. I know Liam is done, but that doesn't help me. The only thing I do know is that Joey knows he scares the shit out of me. So is he trying to bully me out of the money—*my* money? Or does he know that I'm going to think that and he's trying to make me call with a loser?

Suddenly I get this free-fall feeling in my stomach. I look around the room. Joey nods because he thinks I'm looking for information, trying to see if some other player's reaction will give away what cards they had folded. I, of course, am not that savvy and am just surveying the terrain for the best place to puke if it comes to that. I ask for time. That buys me about thirty seconds to think about the situation. For the love of God, I should have tapped on the turn. What a colossal blunder I just made.

Joey is a relatively handsome man. His huge barrel chest, bushy porkchop sideburns, and penchant for wearing a black knit ski hat give him a kind of anonymous longshoreman look. He has not yet been afflicted with any of the classic poker-playing deformities—the gray smoker's complexion, huge fleshy beer belly and backside, or the grim black rings around the eyes—the things that come from sitting in the same place for a month straight.

I'm staring at him in the hopes that his expression might give something away when suddenly a look of sincere empathy comes across his face. "You should have tapped on the turn, huh? I used to make that mistake all the time when I just started playing."

What he's doing now is called "coffeehousing." Playing all Hollywood, trying to talk me into a move. I just don't know which way he's pushing me.

"You know why the American Indian rain dance works, Andy? It works because they don't stop dancing till it rains."

What the hell did that mean?

"You keep dancing, you'll catch me one day," he says, smiling.

Right. Now I want my mommy. If I fold, and he shows me king-jack, I'm going to cry. If I call, and he shows me the ace–4 of clubs . . . I'm really going to cry.

How did I get myself into this? I'm not wondering so much about the specific situation—greed and stupidity got me here, I know that. I'm contemplating the bigger picture, as in how the hell am I sitting in a basement with these freaks about to throw away a month's wages as a freelance journalist, looking for a place to throw up. And then it hits me like a code breaker working on an encryption who was just handed the primer; I'm one of them. I'm the fifth idiot out of the thirty who pour out of the clown car at the circus. I belong here. And beyond that, the wave of nausea that just crested and crashed on top of my head is honestly charging me up. This is absolutely the best I've felt all day.

The dilemma that I am facing now, and all the absurd thoughts and sensations that accompany it, are why an estimated 55 million Americans cram into smoke-filled basements and garages to play poker. And specifically, it's what makes no-limit Texas Hold'em the game of all games.

With only a few seconds left to make my decision, my mind

wanders to the man most responsible for my presence at that table. No, not my father, though I do give him the biological credit, but one of my graduate mathematics professors at Wesleyan University. One day while discussing probability theory, he asked if I ever played poker. I laughed and nodded. The kind doctor taught me many things, but none was more important than the driving directions from Middletown, Connecticut, to the Foxwoods Casino near New London, where I cut my teeth as a poker player under his tutelage.

Once we spent an entire afternoon trying to create a formula to predict the outcome of certain poker situations, in the hopes of constructing an aid to help players decide whether or not to call certain bets. After one of the most beautiful and elegant mathematical explanations ever, he leaned over and said, "And if you're ever truly on the fence, if you've contemplated every bit of evidence and mathematical information, and still you have no idea what to do, you should call."

"Why is that?" I asked.

"Because it's more fun that way."

My time has come with Joey Millman. I push all my chips into the center of the table. "I call."

Joey smiles.

THEORETICAL POKER

The next best thing to playing and winning, is playing and losing.

—A. ALVAREZ,
writer and poker player

Poker, in its most basic form, is a zero-sum game. Without a third party like a house or casino that charges a fee to play in the game, the total sum of money at the table remains constant. When one player loses, another gains. This fact has some interesting consequences when you apply poker to the theory of probability. If two people play in an eternal match, the law of averages dictates that each will eventually receive the exact same hands, in the exact same situations, the exact same number of times. Each will lose at some point with a king-high straight flush to the other's royal straight flush. Each will win holding a hand containing no pair—7 high. Thus, in theory, the wins and losses will eventually equal out, and therefore the players should end up with the exact same number of chips in front of them as they started with. The philosophical crisis has begun. If the theory of probability is correct, and it is, then how is there money to be made at the poker table?

The answer is beautifully simple, wildly complicated, and in its essence, pure Machiavelli and Sun-Tzu; if one plays better than the other, if he out-thinks and out-strategizes, then he will win the most money. Poker isn't about the number of pots you take down, or how fantastic you look winning them (though I do admit to thinking I look really good sometimes). Claiming a pot when you have the best cards isn't enough to make you a winning player. Remember, there is no grand pay scale for holding the best hand. No one gives you a pile of money for drawing a royal straight flush. Some sucker has to pay you off. You have to maximize profits through guile and savvy, eke out every last dollar that your competition is willing to lose to you—and, when you don't have the winning cards, flee as fast as possible.

The key to minimizing losses when you have an inferior hand is recognizing the value of your cards relative to those of your competition. There is no predetermined fine for having a terrible hand. In fact, the stronger your losing cards are, the more money you are likely to part with. That's why the worst hand in poker is the second-best one at the table. When somebody has four aces in a natural game of five-card draw, it is much more monetarily advantageous for his adversary to hold no pair than a full house against him. The no pair is likely to fold right away and lose almost no money, while the full house is bound to misvalue his hand and get caught up in a raising war before he finds out that he's in second place.

One of the most essential components to both minimizing losses and maximizing profits is assessing your competition. Are you in the company of conservative gamblers who fold unless they have great hands? Are they aggressive, tending to overbet? Or are they a group of doubters who will call any wager just to see what you have? This assessment is going to make a huge difference in how you play.

I took my brother to one of the underground poker clubs in New York a few months ago and threw him into a small tournament against some tough players. It was our first time playing together against good competition, so I was eager to show him (show off) how good a player I had become. That was my idea, anyway. But the law of averages had a different vision for that afternoon. I was the third player unceremoniously knocked out of the tournament. This embarrassment took place while my brother—completely unfamiliar with the tournament rules—went on to take third place.

As he continued winning through the afternoon, I kept mumbling to myself that he was getting lucky. Then came this one hand where he called an excellent player's all-in bet with a measly pair of 6s and won. It was a monster call. After the tourney I told him how impressive I thought that was. All he said was, "Come on, it was so obvious that that guy was bluffing." Is it possible that

I had misjudged my brother? Perhaps he had some superhuman ability to read people.

A few months later I showed him an Internet poker site where people buy in on their credit cards and play against each other in a virtual card room. We bought in for a couple of hundred dollars and played a little $20–$40 Hold'em. During one hand some guy raised on his pocket cards before the flop, and we called. He continued to bet and raise every chance he had. After the river card was dealt, my brother and I ended up with a very mediocre hand. So I suggested that we fold. But my brother wasn't having any. He said that he wanted to call the final bet because he thought that guy was bluffing. Now, tell me that my brother can sit across from a guy and get a read on his hand from body language, and I'll say okay, I'll believe that. But say that he can look at a computer screen and, by observing a cartoon drawing, decide that some man in Bulgaria is bluffing by the way he clicked his mouse, I'll be a little more skeptical. As is usually the case with older brothers, nevertheless his point of view prevailed, and we called the bet. The guy showed pocket kings, and we lost another $40. That's when it hit me: my brother is a fine poker player, but more importantly, he's a natural-born skeptic—a quintessential doubter. Perhaps it has something to do with our childhood, I don't know. But that's just the way he is.

As profitable a card player as my brother can sometimes be, skeptics usually get killed in the long run. My poker-playing professor at Wesleyan ran computer simulations of Hold'em hands for almost two months straight. After assigning different poker personalities to a table of seven players, he let the computer play 50,000 hands. The results showed that in only 11 percent of the games did any player fold the winning hand—in other words, a bluff was successful in only about one in ten attempts. Therefore, logic dictates that the skeptic is wasting his money 90 percent of the time. Further statistical analysis showed that consistent calling was even less profitable than that because other players at the table may call as well and have better cards than the skeptic. Therefore, even though a skeptic may catch a bluffer, he can still lose the hand.

Concluding that somebody like my brother is at your table should change the way you approach the game. All those sexy techniques like double bluffs and slow playing that great card players use are going to be ineffective against him. When a player like my brother is in a hand, you must realize that most of the time he's going to call your very last bet just to make sure you have what you claim you do. This turns the game into a showdown competition. Very few hands are going to be won by trying to scare a skeptic off. In the end you're going to have to have the best cards to take the pot.

The easiest way to improve your chances of beating a skeptic is to limit the number of hands you participate in. Only call the first bet if you have premium cards. Poker games are usually decided right after the initial cards are dealt, way before the flop, or draw. If you have the best hand going in, then you have the best chance of winning in the end.

So what's a good starting hand? That depends on what game you're playing. Most of the references I make are to casino games like Omaha, Hold'em, or stud, because I know them best. But the majority of poker played around the world takes place in people's homes and is usually conducted with wild cards or strange draws or flops. Home games have fantastic names like Anaconda, Hello Lavern, Pass the Trash, double draw, double stud, Crazy Pineapple, Night Baseball, Johnny One-Nut, and so on. Even though poker probability gets skewed with so many wild cards and exotic rules ("I call, Tommy, what do you have?" "Five aces!" "Me too, split it up"), the principles of the game remain the same.

A favorite among my friends from college is something called Scungilli. It's a high-low, split-pot game where each player is dealt five cards. Then, like Texas Hold'em and Omaha, a row of five cards comes up (same pattern: first three, then one and one)—but in Scungilli, there are two rows of five community cards, not one. The players are making the best hand out of fifteen cards—that's almost one-third of the deck. I don't care who you are, or what kind of poker you're used to, you have to admit that's kind of ridiculous.

Now, there's not much call for Scungilli in Vegas or at the Winchester Club, yet, as inexperienced as I am, I do play it better than most of the people in my college game. The reason for this is not hard to figure out. I just apply to Scungilli the same math-based logic that I do to other poker games, and I usually come out ahead.

Eric Scoleri is a regular participant in that game. His skills are about average for that group. However, that does not mean that his poker play is unremarkable. In fact, there's something very unique about him. When we play games like Hold'em or five-card draw, where the best hand wins the entire pot, Eric makes money. The single objective of creating the best hand possible makes perfect sense to him. Yet in the ongoing game of Scungilli he's a loser, for one simple reason. As soon as a high-low, split-pot game is called, the elaborate array of possible goals appears to short-circuit his logic (he once said to me, "Now wait a second, I get high and I get low, but doesn't the notion of going both ways seem oxymoronic?"), and he just kind of loses his mind. It doesn't matter what he's dealt, if it's a split-pot game, he plays his hand all the way to the river.

A word here about high-low games, a concept that many who play poker regularly at home find confusing. In these games, there can be two winners: the high hand, as in standard poker, and the player who holds the lowest hand. High hands are the easy part, but some players confuse a "low hand" with a "bad hand"—in other words, they think a low pair, or no pair at all, just five random cards, is a low hand. That's not always true. In fact, one pair is just a very bad high hand. A low hand is five very low cards. The nut low is A, 2, 3, 4, 6 (though it is standard in casino games to have the wheel—A, 2, 3, 4, 5—be the lowest possible hand, even though it is also a straight). High-low games are usually played with five or more cards (for example, in Omaha the player has four pocket cards, plus the five community cards, so nine total). You can use almost any combination of the nine cards to make your best five (you must use two from your hand and three from the board). Therefore, if you want to bet your hand both high and low, you can make two different combinations of five cards. In Scungilli, the odds of going both ways increases dramatically because you're playing with fifteen cards. You can use almost any combination of five to make your high hand, and a different combination of five cards to make your low. It's possible to have a straight flush as your high hand and also make the nut low hand as described above.

These exotic high-low games are easy to get sucked into because there are so many cards to draw to, so many ways to win. Yet there is a way to play them well: try as best you can to never enter a hand without a very good draw to the low.

Any two cards can make the nut high. In a game of Omaha, where the board looks like A♥ 3♦ 6♣ 8♠ 10♣ , any player holding a 2, 4, 7, and 9 has both the nut low and high (A, 2, 3, 4, 6 as a low, and a 10-high straight as a high). In a high-only game of Omaha, very few players call the first bet with a 2, 4, 7, 9. But since it's a high-low game, the 2 and 4 become valuable low cards, so the hand becomes more playable. That's why people make the weirdest hands in split-pot games—small straights, baby flushes; their initial intention is to draw to a low, but they back into a high instead.

Therefore, unless you have a chance to go both ways, you are at a huge disadvantage. You're only competing for half the pot. Eric without fail plays every hand of Scungilli to the bitter end, and usually ends up with the third-best low and fourth-best high hands and loses all the money he won in all the other games. His lack of willingness to part with a fifty-cent ante by folding right away usually costs him $15 per hand. Do that three hands a night, forty nights a year, and that's nearly $2,000 per annum.

Raising the standards you set for yourself to participate in the hand, no matter what the game, is the first step to becoming a profitable player. If you're in a game of seven-card stud, and your first three cards are a king, queen, and a 9 of various suits, even though you have three relatively high cards, it's still an awful, unprofitable starting hand. You're trailing every player that has a lowly pair of 2s or even just a lonely ace. With those cards, the best thing to do is muck your hand right away and wait two minutes for the next game to be dealt.

Position games like Omaha and Texas Hold'em—where the wagering starts in the same place each betting round no matter what action has taken place—require varying starting standards. Depending on where a player is at the table in relation to the dealer (or "button"), he should play different hands. You should play much looser when you are in late position, and much tighter when you are one of the first players to act. A suited 6-7 isn't much of a playable hand when you're under the gun (the first player to act), but if you're the button, and a lot of players have called before you, that hand might even be worth a raise (more callers means more money in the pot, and that makes a mediocre hand more appealing even though there may be stronger hands present in the game).

Once you set yourself a high standard for calling the first bet, you have taken your first step toward becoming a profitable player. It is the poker player's coming-of-age moment. Your motivation for playing the game changes. You realize that fun is no longer your intention at a card table. The search for entertainment is left to the sheep you will fleece. Clever players do enjoy themselves, but it's only an incidental byproduct of a growing mastery of the game.

Now the question moves from what hands to play and when to how long each should be played. There are only a few reasons you should continue playing in a hand. The first, obviously, is if you think you hold the winning cards. That's an excellent justification for continued participation. But what if you've got an incomplete hand, if you're on a draw—how long do you continue to play then? This is where the notion of "pot odds" enters the picture.

Calculating pot odds is the keystone upon which a winning

poker strategy can be built. The first step is to figure out what kind of hand your competition is holding. In most cases it helps to be a catastrophist. Try to apply a worst-case scenario. In a game of Hold'em with five callers and light betting (therefore, you can surmise that no one has a big pocket pair), if the flop looks like J♥ 9♠ 5♦ , you should assume that somebody has made a pair of jacks. Then you can go about calculating out how many outs you have in the hand. If you've played the Q♣ 10♣ , then your outs are as follows: one of three queens (that will make a higher pair), and one of four 8s and four kings (that will give you the nut straight). That's a total of eleven outs.

Since you've seen five out of fifty-two cards (your pocket cards and the flop), you assume that you have an 11 out of 47 chance to catch up on the next card. And since you have two opportunities at those cards (the turn and the river), a good way to estimate your pot odds is to double the number when figuring out your pot odds. You actually have an estimated 22 out of 47, or roughly a 46 percent chance of winning the hand at that moment. This makes you a slight underdog to a pair of jacks. But the question still stands, do you call a bet? Now you compare the size of the pot to your probability of winning it. What you need is enough money in the pot to justify your call. How much is enough? The reward has to justify the risk.

If you flip a fair coin and gamble on it, you're only going to be willing to wager on the outcome if the odds you are receiving represent the probable outcome of the event. Since the odds of the coin landing on heads vs. tails are 50–50, you'd only bet if you were getting at least even money ($1 won for a $1 wager). But, if you were offered fifty cents for a dollar bet, you'd obviously turn the wager down. The risk is not justified because the payout doesn't accurately represent the probability.

So in the hand above—when you are a slight 46 to 54 underdog—you'd only call a $10 bet if there was $11 already at stake. Which, if your opponent is betting $10, is a pretty easy condition to satisfy.

If, in a similar game, you've played the 8♣ 8♥ and the board looks like A♦ J♣ 5♦, then, in calculating your chance of improving, you'd find that you only have two opportunities at two outs (the other 8s), giving you an estimated 4 out of 47 chance of winning the hand. Since you're almost a 12–1 dog, to justify a $10 call, you'd need $120 in the pot.

Once you've mastered counting outs and calculating pot odds, you can then move on to "implied pot odds," where you integrate "what if" scenarios into your thinking. For example, if you are on the nut flush draw with only one card to come, and there isn't enough money in the pot to justify a call. You can throw the final bet on the river into your pot odds calculations because if one of your outs does show up, you are guaranteed to win.

Chances of Drawing Helpful Cards
from a Deck of Forty-Seven Unknown Cards

Scenario	Number of outs	Odds of winning with two cards to come	Odds of winning with one card to come
You have flopped a set but you need quads to win, or an inside draw to a straight flush.	1	4.3%	2.2%
You have a pocket pair, but need to hit your set to win. Or an open-ended draw to a straight flush when somebody has better than a flush.	2	8.4%	4.3%
You have a pair, but need to hit your kicker to win.	3	12.5%	6.5%
You have to hit an inside straight draw to win.	4	16.5%	8.7%
You have a pair and need to hit your kicker or make trips to win.	5	20.4%	10.9%
You have two over cards and need to make a pair to win. Or, you have an open-ended straight draw, but a specific suit will give somebody else a flush.	6	24.1%	13.0%
	7	27.8%	15.2%
You have an open-ended straight draw.	8	31.5%	17.4%
You have a four flush.	9	35.0%	19.6%
	10	38.4%	21.7%
You have a four flush and an over pair in your hand and need to fill the flush or hit your set to win.	11	41.7%	23.9%

Scenario	Number of outs	Odds of winning with two cards to come	Odds of winning with one card to come
You have a four flush and an over card and need to hit either to win.	12	45.0%	26.1%
	13	48.1%	28.3%
	14	51.2%	30.4%
An open-ended straight flush draw.	15	54.1%	32.6%
	16	57.0%	34.8%
	17	59.8%	37.0%
You have an open-ended straight flush draw and an over card and need to hit either to win.	18	62.4%	39.1%
	19	65.0%	41.3%
	20	67.5%	43.5%

Once you understand how to count outs, you'll have a better idea of what is a good starting hand. If you are playing seven-card stud against a single opponent, and your first three cards are the 2, 6, and 7 of clubs, most amateurs will call the first bet because they have a flush draw. But most of the time, the ante will not produce the pot odds necessary for the unlikely outcome of two of the next four cards being the clubs you need to win. Once you understand pot odds, you would fold those openers without calling one bet.

An essential concept to calculating pot odds is trying to figure out what cards the other players are holding. You do this by reading body language for some sort of tell, and deducing what possible hands they could have played given their actions (calling or raising) from their position at the table. If you add an ability to read players to only playing premium starting hands and calculating pot odds, you are bound to become a profitable card player.

Another key to maximizing profits is to realize why you bet. To simplify a very complicated concept, there are basically two purposes to betting. The first is fairly self-evident. You want other people's money. Therefore, if you genuinely believe that your hand is the best, you want to bet and raise so you can increase the amount of money contained within the pot.

The other reason you bet—and raise—is to narrow the field. You eliminate some, or all, of the competition and therefore have a better chance of winning. It's important to remember that these two concepts are often counterproductive. The more people you play against, the more money there is at stake. But at the same time, the more people participating in a hand, the less likely it is that you'll hold the winning hand. That's why there's an art to betting and why there is almost never one correct maneuver in any poker hand.

Sometimes, though you hold a great hand, you never initiate a bet. This is called "slow playing"; you're holding back to keep as many people in the hand as possible. Let's say you're in a game of Texas Hold'em. You call a raise with [4♣][4♦]. The flop comes [4♥][4♠][3♣]. You've got quads. Very sexy. Now, unless somebody has pocket threes, any big bet or raise from you early on may scare off your competition and win you just the ante. That's not the worst scenario, but it's important to keep in mind that your job is not to simply take the pot, you're trying to make the most money possible out of this divine gift. So you play possum. It helps to be playing against aggressive competition who overbet their hands, but regardless, you just check and call until the final bet. Why not let somebody make a straight, flush, or full house? They're drawing practically dead to your four of a kind, after all. Let the field catch up while building the pot. Then depending on your position, you'll either raise or check-raise in the later rounds.

There is, of course, a down side to slow playing; by putting more money in the pot, you're giving the other players more reason to chase you down. And sometimes you're going to get caught. Let's say you were dealt [Q♦][Q♥] (known as the "Siegfried & Roy," for obvious reasons). You raise, and get a few callers. The flop comes [Q♣][3♠][4♥]. You now have three queens (often referred to as "six tits"), the top set. This is a great hand to slow-play because there are very few ways somebody can catch up to you. Might as well let the guy with ace-king catch his best card and think he's a winner. But if the flop comes [10♣][J♣][Q♣], that's a terrible hand to slow-play because there are so many cards that can hurt you. You might be dead already. And if the turn is another club or straight card, your three queens become almost unplayable. In this case you have to play the hand as fast as possible and hope you scare off any potential winners or at least make it expensive for them to see the next card.

(Just a note here about check-raising: there are some home games in which check-raising is looked down upon or even banned. No offense intended to those practitioners of that rule, but it goes against what betting is all about. Not being able to play deceptively in a poker game is absurd. Doyle Brunson said that playing poker without check-raising is like playing football without the forward pass. You have to be able to deviate from the obvious to play effectively. Otherwise, poker becomes a purely positional game. If somebody has to act before you in a game where check-raising is banned, they are at a phenomenal disadvantage. If they choose not to bet, it can only mean that they have a weak hand. Without the possibility that they are setting a trap, any aggressive bet from you has a great chance of winning the pot.)

In a game with limited betting structures, *when* to bet is the most significant part of wagering. But in a game without limits, *how much* you bet is the most important decision you'll have to make. I played in my first high-stakes no-limit game about three years ago for an article I was writing for *Esquire*. It was a $10,000 buy-in at the Winchester Club. I had a little no-limit experience back then, but I'd never played with such an intimidating sum of money.

One of the great mistakes you can make in poker is playing in a game where the stakes are over your head. If you start thinking about the actual worth of all those clay chips, it knocks you off your game. I tend to play scared and tight when losses hurt much more than I am accustomed to.

In one of the early hands, I played a 10-8 off suit, and I flopped the nut 10-high straight. There was about $30 in the pot at the time. After the flop, some guy bet $10 into me. At that point all I could think was that I had the nuts. I was going to win the hand. Without a second's thought, I raised him by betting my entire $10,000. Now, there was absolutely no way this guy was ever going to call a ten grand wager with $40 in the pot unless he had the exact same hand I did. So he folded. It's a perfect example of how not to maximize profits. With so little money at stake, I could have just waited out the hand by betting small sums and won a few extra dollars. I basically won the smallest amount possible, and that's just bad poker.

PROBABILITY, STATISTICS, AND RELIGION

It's unlucky to be superstitious.

—DAVE ENTELES,
card player

I have never met anyone who would admit to being bad in bed. No one describes themselves as a terrible lover. And yet a huge percentage of the population is completely clueless when it comes to sex. So what accounts for the contradiction? Well, for starters, a realistic sense of self. The same thing can be found among poker players. Very few people who play the game think they play badly. Still, at every card table in the world, there are regular participants whose skill and understanding are almost nonexistent, and whose long-term negative result leaves no room for doubt. This dichotomy exists in poker due mostly to ignorance and ego. My friend Dave Enteles is a perfect example.

Dave Enteles is a friend of mine from college, an occasional participant in my original Vassar poker game. David is a nice guy, very funny, quick-witted, with a unique aesthetic appeal that you could only understand if you pictured a white Chris Rock with Bruce Willis's hairline. Yet his most striking characteristic is that Dave Enteles is a terrible poker player. He is perhaps the worst I have ever seen. Anecdotes and statistics cannot do justice to the level of awfulness with which he conducts his play.

If he were new to the game, or was perhaps suffering from some emotional disorder, his absence of card skill would be understandable. But he is, by all clinical definitions, sane. And what makes his feebleness seem almost intentional is that he has been playing poker for more than ten years now. Ten years, and yet somehow this self-proclaimed "King of Cards" still finds it necessary to have a list of the ranks of hands placed next to him at all times.

His card strategy is akin to the U.S. exit strategy in Vietnam. He has none. Absolutely none. It's shocking. His play is completely devoid of all rational thought. To give an example, I was once "sweating his hand" (playing along with him, looking at his cards) and watched him call the final bet with an ace high in a game of seven-card stud when the person who bet was showing a pair of nines on the board. I asked him why he called when there was no way he could win, and Dave replied, "I didn't want anybody to think that I had bad cards."

What makes his story more interesting is that during the first half of 1999, Dave won more money playing in my regular Tuesday-night game than anybody else, including me. The only word to describe him at a card table during that time is lucky, and I don't believe in luck. He played as if he was possessed. Guided by God. Surrounded by an all-powerful winning force.

There are a lot of habitual poker players who are very lonely. For those individuals, the game functions as a social life. It gets them out of the house and puts them among people. Most of these lonely card players love to talk, and a poker game is often the only time when their verbal interaction is not limited to talking to their pet.

Of course, just because these people love to talk, it doesn't make them interesting. Some players are proud parents or grandparents who constantly boast about their offspring's accomplishments. Some are braggarts who can't stop talking about how big they play, or who they play with. The worst kind of conversationalists are the ones who regale the table over and over again with variations of the "bad beats" they've taken in their lives. They'll tell you how they flopped the nut flush last month while on vacation in Mississippi and lost $80 to some guy who hit the only card in the deck on the river that could make his straight flush. Every bar room and card house in the world is filled with bad beat stories. These people don't understand that every card player has taken bad beats, they just don't talk about it. But Dave is special, and therefore, I will tell a bad beat story of my very own.

My college friends and I are playing seven card stud. I am dealt "rolled up 7s" (all three of my cards—two down and one up—were 7s). Dave has garbage, something like a rainbow (no matching suits) 3, 6, 9. But, as he explained after the game, "My spider sense was tingling, what can I say, I had a very good feeling about the hand." So he calls my maximum bet. The rest of the players in the game have come to know me as a fairly serious card player, and thus fold. By fifth street (the fifth card), I've got a pair of kings showing, which, when combined with the three 7s I was dealt at the beginning of the game, gives me a full house. The fact that I've got a pair of kings showing, and that I've been betting my nuts off each turn, should convey that I have a rather strong hand. But again, as Dave explained during the postmortem sermonette that I delivered on how disgusting his play was, when I paired my kings, that's when he "knew he had me."

At that point in the game, Dave managed to cull a pair of 6s from his jumble of meaningless cards. That's it. He had no possible flush draw, there was some weird back-door straight draw, but even so, that was completely useless as I already had a full house.

So I bet again, as I have been all hand, and he calls. In hindsight, Dave says that he misplayed by not raising my full house with his pair of 6s, but "no one can play perfectly," he reminds me. Now, even if he had put me on a measly two pair—kings and a pair matched with one of my down cards—he still had only one small pair and he didn't even have an "over card" (in this case the ace was the only card higher than my kings) to draw to so he could make a higher two pair. And if the situation was not grim enough, one of the other players' up cards at the beginning of the game was the third 6, so Dave had no chance of making quads. To win, he needed one thing and one thing only. With his last two cards, he had to draw two of the three 9s left in the deck. That way, his 9s full of 6s would best my 7s full of kings.

The odds of this happening are very simple to calculate. First he must figure out how many cards he has not seen yet. So far, Dave's been privy to his own five cards, my three up cards, and the four up cards that the other players folded after the first bet of the game. Subtracting those twelve from the fifty-two cards in the deck gives him forty unknown cards to draw to (we know he's only got 38 unknown cards because we know what my two down cards were, but he doesn't). Since all three remaining 9s were "live" (they had not been seen yet), Dave's odds of getting one of the 9s on the sixth card were $3/40 = .075$ or 7.5%. After that round he would have seen two more cards (the up cards dealt to each of us), leaving him with only thirty-eight unknown cards, but he'll have one less 9 to draw to since he got dealt one of the three. So the odds of him improving on the last card would be $2/38 = .052$, or almost 5 percent.

But it got worse. On sixth street, the up card Dave was dealt was obviously one of his nines, but I was also dealt a nine. That gave him one lonely nine to draw to win the game. He had an almost impossible 1 in 38 chance of winning, or roughly 2.5 percent. And, of course, he hit his only out on the river.

I don't tell this story to berate Dave. I'm not angry at that son of a bitch. I spin this yarn to illustrate a point. The odds of him going runner-runner (drawing two necessary cards in a row) to win the pot were an incredible $(3/40) \times (1/38) = .001$. Simply put, he had roughly a one-in-a-thousand chance of winning. And if that doesn't sound like a hopeless enough situation, keep in mind that I actually had a better chance of improving my hand than he did. I still had a 7 and two kings to draw to. All told, after fifth street, he was something like a two-thousand-to-one underdog.

There wasn't nearly enough money in the pot to justify him drawing to such astronomical odds, so he should have folded. But he did win the hand, so it's hard to reach any other conclusion than he did the right thing by playing. That dichotomous appraisal of the situation is the essence of gambling. To figure out whether he really did the right thing or not, we first must understand a few concepts: probability, statistics, and religion.

In the absence of any mathematical explanation, one thing is for certain; if you engage in games of chance long enough, the experience is bound to affect the way you see God. Successfully draw to an inside straight three hands in a row, and you've got to be blessed. But if you're the person drawn out on, the one whose trip aces just got snapped for the third time, you will go home feeling cursed. It's the nature of poker.

That's why there are so many tales of poker players changing religions in the middle of a game. I once saw an Episcopal minister who plays regularly at my card club swear to devote more time reading the Torah after having pocket kings crushed two hands in a row. Moments after issuing his statement, Chip (Holy Chip to those who know him) suddenly went on a five-grand tear. It is the cruel, unimpassioned distribution of the cards that gives rise to the notion of the poker gods. Whether you are religious or an atheist, the poker gods are as real as you let them be. And for those six months in 1999—when he was winning almost every hand—the poker gods were completely at peace with Dave Enteles. So there's the religious aspect of his winning streak; now we must consider the theory of probability.

Yes, it's true that there is a lot of *feel* to the game of poker, and a lot of idiosyncratic subtleties like body language that make your hand transparent to a skilled opponent. But all strategy and pop psychology aside, poker is in its essence a mathematical game.

The theory of probability is an area of mathematics created in the mid-1600s by two French mathematicians, Pierre de Fermat and Blaise Pascal. A gambler's dispute was brought to their attention by a French nobleman who himself was fascinated by gambling. The nobleman had found a contradiction in a dice game that had become popular around France at that time. He wanted to make sure that the payout the house was offering gamblers represented the actual probabilities of the events occurring.

In the game the nobleman played, a gambler rolled a pair of six-sided dice twenty-four times. If he rolled a double 6 in that time, the gambler would be paid even money on whatever he wagered. The nobleman wanted to know if this was an equitable payout or not. This question led to a collaboration between Fermat and Pascal, and from it, the basic principles of probability theory were composed for the first time.

While Fermat and Pascal were nearing the completion of their study, they discovered something very interesting; the theory of probability that they were creating was just a mathematical framework for understanding and predicting random phenomena. It was not a definitive proof like "if A=B and B=C, then A=C" where an absolute, concrete conclusion is reached.

In a roundtable discussion on probability theory that I organized, NYU math professor Marco Avellaneda explained the difference between a proof and a theory:

> A proof is a mathematical argument intended to verify whether a statement is true or false. Something like: Prove that the sum of the first N numbers is N times (N+1) divided by 2. A theory is a framework for thinking about scientific problems. To qualify as

a theory, it must provide a new blueprint of ideas that makes problems appearing difficult, become simpler. A perfect example is how the theory of gravity explains elegantly the orbits of planets around the sun.

The theory of probability is merely a scientific asset that provides a window from which the future can be glimpsed. However, the vast array of possible outcomes leads to many possible futures, and nobody can say which one will come to be. Flip a coin once, and probability theory will tell you that you have a 50-50 chance of landing on heads. But will it? That's the question, and it's one that's better left to philosophy rather than science.

In this way the theory of probability is very much like a religion. There are some factual components derived from math and science, but the greatest necessity in accepting the theory turns out to be faith. Probability theory is simply an ever-present phenomenon that governs all things related to chance. Even though mathematicians accept it, they cannot prove it. But that doesn't bring its existence into question. The theory of probability is an enduring certainty. Its very existence conjures billion-dollar hotels out of the Mojave desert, allows the sovereign citizens of Monte Carlo to live a tax-free life, and causes the U.S. divorce rate to skyrocket among people who gamble frequently.

The first conclusion reached when probability theory is applied to life is, "Nothing that is mathematically possible is wholly improbable." I have an overweight Newfoundland dog named Calamity who, by any measure of intelligence, would be considered a dope. In her nine years of life I have managed to teach her seven words of the English language. One is her name; the other six are synonyms for food. Whenever I leave a deck of cards out in my apartment, she has a penchant for taking the top card in her mouth and bringing it over to me. Some dogs instinctively jump into icy rivers to save children, bringing me cards is just Calamity's thing. Don't ask me why. After a card game at my house one night, I was seated in the living room with a few stragglers, talking about the game. I saw that Calamity was eyeing the deck of cards in the other room, so I said, "Calamity, bring me the 7 of clubs." Sure enough, a minute later, Calamity showed up with a card in her mouth. I took it from her and turned it over. Neither of us had any idea what it was, but it turned out to be the 7 of spades.

My friends were shocked. "I know," I said, "she's got trouble recognizing the suits. We're working on it." The point is, over a long enough period, anything that has a chance of happening will happen. Seated long enough at a card table, even Dave Enteles is going to stumble upon a fantastic winning streak. So, a 10-high straight flush is a monster hand in a natural game of five-card draw. It's almost unbeatable, but some poor sucker loses with that hand every day.

Another important concept to keep in mind is that statistics do not always have a practical application to human life. That is to say, they are not always pertinent. The theory of probability becomes more meaningful the more times you participate in a game of chance. If you're dealing with a tiny number of trials, your results may be completely skewed. Let's use flipping a coin as an example. If a coin is flipped two times, the assumption is that the experiment will result with one head and one tail. But in fact, the possible results of the trial are more complicated.

The possible results of flipping a coin twice can be expressed in the following table:

Result	Probability of Result
HH	25%
TT	25%
HT	25%
TH	25%

To find out the chances of arriving at a mixed result (head-tail or tail-head), you just add up the two probabilities. This table illustrates that you are just as likely to arrive at the mixed head-tail result as you are a non mixed one. Each has a 50-50 chance of occurring. But if we double the number of flips in the trial, we see that the odds of a 50-50 result change.

Results	Probability of Result
HHHH	6.25%
HHHT	6.25%
HHTH	6.25%
HHTT	6.25%
HTHH	6.25%
HTHT	6.25%
HTTH	6.25%
HTTT	6.25%
THHH	6.25%
THHT	6.25%
THTH	6.25%
THTT	6.25%
TTHH	6.25%
TTHT	6.25%
TTTH	6.25%
TTTT	6.25%

The odds of getting a true 50-50 result have actually fallen to 37.5 percent, but—and this is extremely important—the chances of getting a result closer to the expected outcome, that being 50-50, have greatly increased. In the first experiment, the chances of getting a result that was all heads or all tails were even money. But when we double the number of trials, those chances fall to 12.5 percent.

Here are the results of an experiment where a coin is flipped fifty times:

TTHHHTHTHHHHTHTHHHHHTTHT

TTHTHTTTTHHTHHTTTTHHHTTHTT

There are twenty-five heads and twenty-five tails—a perfect result. But, if you were only flipping the coin twice, we would have gotten a skewed result of two tails. Also, out of the first twenty flips, fourteen were heads. If you spent your whole life flipping a coin, you would find that it landed on heads 50 percent of the time. Flip it only twice, and you only have a one in two chance at arriving at the same result. The more chances you take, the more hands you play, the more likely it is that the numbers will hold true. But in a short period, anything can happen.

That is usually the biggest mistake a gambler will make. Some people try to predict a pending outcome by paying attention to the past. Some gamblers will lose a bet, then double up on the next wager, thinking that the odds are in their favor or that the game somehow owes them something. Think of it this way: it's true that the odds of a 13 being spun on a roulette wheel twice in a row are 1 in 1,444 (38 × 38). But after the first thirteen hits, the odds of the next spin landing on 13 are only 1 in 38.

Cliff Hurvich, a professor of mathematics at Columbia University, put it this way:

> If you study the numbers that have come up recently on a roulette wheel, you are very likely to see patterns. Finding patterns is something humans are very good at. It's an important survival skill. In the case of the roulette wheel, though, the patterns we think we see are really just illusions. They will have no tendency to continue in future spins of the wheel. Probability

theory tells us what is likely to happen on the average if we spin the wheel many times. But there is no such thing as a "law of averages" that says that if we have been losing recently (in a fair game, let's say), we will soon have to start winning again so that our losses will even out. In fact, if a gambler plays in a fair game repeatedly, the number of rounds they should expect to wait for their fortune to get back to what it was in the first place is a very large number indeed: infinity.

The longest anomalous gambling streak I've ever heard of took place on a roulette table in Monte Carlo. I was told that the ball landed on black twenty-eight times in a row. European wheels have only one space—a green 0—that is not red or black (American tables have 0 and 00), so the odds of spinning black is 18/37, or 48.6 percent of the time. The odds of hitting black twice in a row are therefore $18/37 \times 18/37$ or $(18/37)^2$, which happens 23.7 percent of the time. The exponent represents the number of trials. So the odds of twenty-eight blacks in a row are $(18/37)^{28}$ or .0000000017 percent—roughly 600 million to one. Any idiot who saw ten blacks in a row and thought they had easy money by betting red lost the next eighteen spins. Thus, "Nothing that is mathematically possible is wholly improbable."

A gambler walks into a casino to place one single bet. Almost half the time that person is going to walk out a winner. This is true for almost any game. Play one hand of poker against Doyle Brunson, and you've got a decent shot at coming out on top. This is a phenomenon known as "small population probability." The reason casinos stay in business and Doyle lives in a multimillion-dollar house is that they deal in large populations. Doyle plays tens of thousands of hands of poker a year. The more hands he plays, the more likely the statistics hold true, and the more likely he will win.

That's why the casino makes money. The house has a statistical advantage in every casino game. The house's advantage in roulette comes from the pay-out schedule. When you bet a number on an American roulette board, you have a 1 in 38 chance of winning. But when the gambling gods smile and you hit, your payout is only 35–1. This creates an inequality.

Think about it rationally. One in 38 implies that if you spun the wheel thirty-eight times and bet $1 on the number 4 every time, you would win once during that session. And for your troubles, you'd be paid a grand total of $36 (the $35 you won plus the $1 you bet). So the law of averages held up, and you didn't win a thing. In fact, you spent $38 to win $36. No matter what strategy you employ, you are going to be in a losing position. Every civilian in a casino is in the same boat. That's because of the discrepancy in the risk-to-reward ratio.

To figure out how a gambler is supposed to fare making $100 worth of bets is pretty easy. The chances of a winning are 1 in 38, the payout is 35 to 1, and the chances of losing are 37 out of 38.

The explanation for the following formula—though it makes perfect sense—is kind of complicated. So let's just say that after a lot of chalk has been pressed against a blackboard, the formula looks like:

$$35 \times (1/38) - 1 \times (37/38) = -.0526.$$

This means that the expected return on one hundred $1 bets on roulette is minus $5.26. Thus, the house has a distinct 5.26 percent advantage.

The house's advantage from blackjack comes from the fact that if both players bust, the house still wins. In baccarat and Pai-Gow, the house simply takes a percentage of a player's wins. These are cold, hard facts that make the gambling business a sure thing for the house.

This is why casino owner Benny Binion was such a renegade when he adopted high limit policies at his tables. If you wanted to bet $100 but the limit was only $10, then you'd have to make the limit wager ten times to make the bet you wanted. But if the table maximum is $100, then you only have to make one bet, and that cuts into the house's edge.

If we assume that a blackjack player employs a reasonably well-thought-out strategy that gives the house a 49-to-51-percent edge, here is an explanation of his expected return in relation to the number of hands he plays:

Number of hands	Chances of Being Ahead	Chances of Being Even
5	48.12	0
10	35.26	24.56
15	46.86	0
20	37.70	17.54
25	45.97	0
30	38.49	14.36
35	45.25	0
40	38.77	12.43
45	44.63	0
50	38.84	11.11
55	44.07	0
60	38.80	10.13
65	43.56	0
70	38.69	9.37
75	43.10	0
80	38.54	8.75
85	42.66	0
90	38.37	8.23
95	42.25	0
100	38.19	7.80

Notice the difference between even/odd number of games above. This is because it's not possible to be perfectly even after an odd number of games.

That gambler has a 48.12 percent chance of being ahead after five hands. But those odds drop to 42.25 percent after playing ninety-five. The more hands you play, the more likely it is you are going to lose.

That's why poker players don't consider what they do gambling. If you're playing in a home game, there is no house to have the advantage. No money comes off the table. Each player has the same statistical chance of getting the best cards as the other. Casinos make a little bit of money through poker by charging a fee known as the rake or chop. A standard chop for a $10–$20 game of stud or Hold'em is $5 per half hour. Also, most card rooms are deep in the bowels of the casino, forcing a winning poker player to walk past as many game tables as possible. It's very common for some guy to grind out a $300 win over a number of hours at a midlevel poker game and then lose it on two rolls of the dice at the craps table in a matter of seconds.

The last thing to keep in mind is that the theory of probability has no idea what game you are playing. The odds of being dealt any specific poker hand (any combination of five cards) is 1 in 2,598,960. You have the same chances of being dealt a royal straight flush in spades as you do the 7 of hearts, 6 of spades, 5 of diamonds, 3 of clubs, and 2 of hearts. The only difference is that the rules of poker have created a hierarchy of hand ranks that makes one result more appealing than another. That hierarchy was created by a statistical analysis that observed what group of combinations is more likely to occur.

Odds against Holding Various Hands on the Deal

Quantity	Hand	Odds against drawing
4	Royal straight flush	649,739 to 1
36	Straight flush	64,973 to 1
624	Four of a kind	4,164 to 1
3,744	Full house	693 to 1
5,108	Flush	508 to 1
10,200	Straight	254 to 1
54,912	Three of a kind	46 to 1
123,552	Two pairs	20 to 1
1,098,240	One pair	1.25 to 1
1,302,540	No pair	1 to 1

Leif Jensen, a professor of probability and statistics at Columbia University, pointed out that so much could be concluded about poker from the theory of probability.

- The first card is equally likely to be any of the cards.

- The second card is equally likely to be any of the cards, except the first one already dealt, and so on.

Then you analyze the data and come up with an observation like, There is a 3,744/2,598,960 chance of having a full house. At any one time you either get a full house or you don't. So there's your statistical conclusion. What to make of this figure of

3,744/2,598,960, and why you get the cards you do when you do, is a philosophical question.

Since the human life span is far from the infinite period it would take to experience even odds, there will be those individuals who, through their lifetime, will for no rational reason simply defy probability. They are not special or superhuman, they have no telekinetic power or extrasensory perception. They just seem to be overlooked by the theory of probability. I know in my heart that if Dave Enteles plays 2,598,960 hands of poker in his life, he's going to get way more than his fair share of 3,744 full houses. Do you want to know why? Well, so do I. Please feel free to write him at: **KingDave@Pokernation.net**. I'm sure he'd be glad to let you know what it feels like to be special.

BENNY BINION
AND THE WORLD SERIES OF POKER

*The game exemplifies the worst aspects of
capitalism that have made our country so great.*

—WALTER MATTHAU

Benny Binion was the kind of fragile kid who would have gotten
beaten up a lot in grammar school. It wasn't his fault; he just had
bad lungs that frequently filled with liquid, which brought on re-
curring bouts of pneumonia. If his doctors were bookmakers, the
over/under on his life expectancy might have been set at ten years
old; and the odds of him living to see his teenage years, probably
four to one against.

The Texas school system in 1910 was not a particularly hos-
pitable place for kids with such afflictions. Maybe that's why
Benny never went to school one day in his life. Not one. "There's
more than one kind of education, and maybe I prefer the one I
got," Benny once said in an interview. "I suppose if I had it to do

over again, I would almost certainly be a gambler again, because there's nothing else an ignorant man can do."

Benny Binion was many things to many people; father, philanthropist, horse trader, bootlegger, numbers runner, casino operator, tax evader, cardplayer, and convicted murderer. But more than anything, he was a gambler. In 1946, his first year in Las Vegas, Benny lost about $400,000 playing poker. It was a pretty inauspicious start for the man who would eventually become the greatest influential force on poker's development into the multibillion-dollar-a-year business that it is today.

When he was born, in Grayson County, Texas, in 1904, Benny Binion's future did not seem particularly bright. Finding no medical solution to his problem, his family came up with the quintessential 1900s Texan treatment for his frail respiratory system; they put him on a horse and sent him to work endless days in the summer sun with his father. They must have concluded that no matter the result, Benny would be better off figuring out whether he was going to live or die early on. Their experiment worked, and by the time he was thirteen, the fresh air and cowboy's life had turned him into a robust, healthy horse trader.

Aside from allowing him to grow into a strong young man, the real beauty of Benny's lifestyle was the opportunity it gave him to learn about things far beyond the scope of mules and wagons. When they were out on the trail, most traders would make camp at the same watering holes, ten to fifteen of them gathering at a time. You put that many men together with very little else to do but drink whiskey and smoke, and a card game is bound to break out. At night the traders would play poker by the campfire, and they were serious games; some would bet their horses when they ran out of cash. Benny watched it all, learning as much about compulsions and what people wanted out of their recreational time as he did about the game.

Benny also got to see firsthand the impact that losing had on people. His father was not particularly good at cards, which translated into him not being particularly good at dealing with money. So when Benny was about fourteen, he was burdened with the responsibility of being the primary source of income for his family. It was an obligation that he took very seriously.

In 1922 Binion moved to El Paso, where he worked laying gravel in parking lots. It was there that he began his lifelong entanglement with the law. It didn't take long for him to realize that a booth on one of the lots he worked on doubled as a bootlegger's front for selling alcohol. Benny studied how the transaction went down, then drove across the border to Oklahoma, picked up a few bottles of whiskey, and mimicked what the bootleggers did. Everybody just assumed that he had some connection to the smugglers working the lot.

Benny never saw what he was doing as a criminal act. The fact that his actions conflicted with the law was irrelevant; he was just giving people what they wanted. "Making folks happy, what the hell is wrong with that?" he used to say. And if he got rich doing it, so much the better. There were, however, some sizable drawbacks to being a bootlegger at that time. Jail and violent competition were a very real part of doing business. Benny took it all in stride and adapted quickly, learning to protect what was his (there is a story about him throttling ten men with the detached bumper of his car after a traffic accident) and to roll with the punches by making the most of any situation (when he was in jail, he managed to sell confiscated alcohol to a few judges in town). It was only when he had become a well-known trafficker with a high-profile reputation that he thought twice about his choice of occupation. After his second conviction for bootlegging, Benny swore to a judge that if he could get out of serving more time in jail, he'd give up smuggling forever. They agreed, and Benny moved back to the Dallas area, where he kept his word and never sold bootlegged whiskey again. Instead, he started running numbers and began his life as a gambler.

Dallas's upper class was one of the few sections of American society that shrugged off the Great Depression. Oil was still pumping out of the ground, and people were still paying for it, so they had no need for Roosevelt's New Deal. What the community did want was entertainment, and they were willing to pay almost anything for it. Recognizing this fact was, in a sense, the beginning of Benny Binion's life work. Like when Roger Clemens threw his first baseball and thought, "That was fun, and I'm pretty good at it, maybe I'll do it again," Binion's moment of destiny was starting a floating craps game out of a hotel room. Everything he had learned in his entire life led to that moment. There were lots of other craps games, other gambling halls all over town, but it took no time at all for Benny's to become the most popular. He was great at running a game, and the reasons for that were pretty simple. First, he was known for being an honest criminal. And he brought that reputation to his game by making sure it was run as fairly as possible. The other thing he did was set higher table limits than anybody else around. That's it. That's been the not-so-secret ingredient to Benny Binion's success his whole life: Let people gamble as much as they wanted, and deal a straight game. A few years later the same formula would make him millions of dollars as well as a Vegas legend.

The success of the game and the money that flowed from it led Benny to another one of his trademark characteristics: he spent so much time around gamblers that he got to see the very worst aspects of human nature, and consequently he developed what he once called "safety impulses." The Binion trademark was lots of muscle. He hired many men with weapons to watch over all his games. And to protect himself from the protection, Benny always carried three guns: two .45 automatics and a Smith and Wesson .38 that he kept in his jacket pocket. And there was usually a sawed-off shotgun hidden somewhere in his car for good measure.

Binion showed on a number of occasions the wisdom in the old adage, It's better to have a gun and not need it than to need one and not have it. In 1931 he discharged the S&W .38 into the neck of a fellow bootlegger. The two were just sitting on a log, talking about business, when the man made a sudden move for his pocket. He didn't pull anything out or make a threat, the guy just reached into his jacket. Benny had heard a great deal about this man's reputation for being lethal with a knife, so he took the sudden move as a precursor to a violent act. Benny rolled off the log, pulled the .38, fired, and dropped the man without a second thought.

To anyone with no knowledge of the characters involved and mitigating circumstances, the facts surrounding the killing did not paint Binion in a favorable light. Two men walked into the woods, stopped to discuss business, and when one of them reached into his pocket, the other shot him dead. There was a large knife found in the victim's jacket, but Binion had not given him the time to pull it out. Those were the facts a prosecutor presented to a jury, and on their merit, a collection of Benny Binion's peers found him guilty of first-degree murder.

Texas was famed for executions, particularly around the time of its centennial, but Binion stumbled upon a sympathetic judge who knew a great deal about the victim's past, and Binion was only ordered to serve two years in jail. Moments later the judge suspended the sentence, and Benny walked from the courthouse a free man.

It took just five years for Benny to discharge the .38 again. This time it was into the torso of Ben Frieden, a local gangster and competitor of Binion's. He died as a result of the wound. Benny's son and protégé, Ted, once described the event. "I was told that Dad was walking down the street and Ben called him over to his car. Ben was smiling. As Dad came up real close to him Ben upped his gun; he'd had it hidden behind the door. Dad threw up his arm, I guess instinctively as if he could stop the bullet, and Ben Frieden shot him in the armpit. He grabbed the cylinder of Ben Frieden's gun so it wouldn't turn and wouldn't shoot again." Moments after, Ben Frieden was dead.

(Ted himself would eventually die under extremely suspicious circumstances. In 1998 he overdosed on prescription drugs. His death was almost ruled a suicide, until the authorities realized that the $5 million worth of silver Ted had buried on his ranch was missing. Ted's girlfriend Sandy Murphy and a male accomplice were found guilty of first-degree murder in the spring of 2000.)

Benny Binion had ended the life of another gangster, but since the second time the victim actually had a weapon in his hand, he was found to have acted in self-defense, and the prosecutor chose not to bring the case before a jury.

That was what Dallas was in those days—a vice-driven underground economy, propelled by big oil money, run by brutal men, and with seemingly no end in sight. Petty gang wars over turf and reputations broke out across the city, costing many of Binion's friends and rivals their lives. When the bodies began to appear all over town, authorities and gangsters alike began to look for a usual suspect, and because of his reputation as a killer, Benny Binion was always it. When Mildred Noble, wife of gambler Herbert Noble, was killed by a car bomb meant for her husband, everybody assumed that Benny had been behind the assassination attempt.

Vengeful threats and ultimatums were often volleyed back and forth between racketeers in the aftermath of violent action, but most of the time it was just posturing and harsh rhetoric. But Mildred Noble's death was different. Herbert Noble was a tough man with a notorious temper. Binion knew it was going to be a real problem. Not only was he concerned about his own well-being, but he feared for the safety of his loved ones as well. So, shortly after the incident, he decided to take his family to Las Vegas for a long vacation.

Herbert Noble did live up to his famous reputation. A report filed by a police officer who visited Noble's house to question him on a topic unrelated to the Binion matter stated that Noble was discovered undertaking a very curious action. A licensed pilot,

Noble was found attaching bombs to a plane that he had purchased. The police officer also confiscated a handwritten flight plan leading directly to Binion's ranch. When word of this reached Benny Binion, he decided to make Las Vegas his permanent home.

When Binion arrived in town, Vegas was a gangster's paradise. Wise guys and bosses like Benjamin "Bugsy" Siegel and Moe Dalitz still ran their joints. It was considered open country. At least twenty-four crime families had a small interest in Vegas enterprises. Each was allowed to chisel and skim from the profits as long as no one got greedy or caught.

The violence of the next generation of mobsters (those portrayed in the movie *Casino*) had not arrived yet, so there was still a sense of innocence and naïveté floating in the desert air. Citizens actually felt safer with the Mafia so heavily involved in the city's affairs. They were like a second police force. In those exciting, early days in Las Vegas, it was said that nobody got killed who wasn't supposed to.

Binion's first endeavor in Nevada was the Las Vegas Club, a casino that he and a partner named J. Kell Houssells, Sr., would run together. Their partnership was a perfect combination. Houssells was already a big-time player in Vegas real estate, gambling, and entertainment. Benny brought the missing ingredient: pure gambling expertise. The first thing they did was set higher betting limits than most of the other casinos in town. This took away some of the casino's edge and therefore made the establishment more gambler-friendly. It was a move that contradicted almost every axiom of casino operation and profitability.

For all the romance, glimmer, and glamour of Las Vegas, the city is built upon a foundation of pure mathematics. Each establishment, from the billion-dollar Bellagio down to the Howard Johnson's Hotel and Casino, operates on one simple principle: the theory of probability. Every gambler at every table has an expected loss of money for every hour played and dollar wagered. This doesn't mean everybody will lose. Vegas wouldn't be much of a draw if that were true. It's just that they are mathematically supposed to lose. An individual's success or failure means nothing to the casino. They are only concerned with the big picture. Over time, the more people who gamble, the more money that is wagered, the more the house will eventually win. Every casino knows this; it's the law. Therefore, the ambition of the casino is not to separate the players from their money—the house advantage built into every game takes care of that—it is to get as many people as possible to play as many games as possible for as long as possible.

Every tiny aspect of each hotel's construction is geared toward that end. The architect lays out the lobby design so the guest must walk through the casino to do just about everything. If they want to go to the pool, they pass the gaming tables. If they want to eat a meal, buy a newspaper, or just check in, they must stroll through the casino every time. That's why the room service in Las Vegas is so awful. The management wants you out and about. You're not going to lose much money sitting in the bath. For every square foot of casino a guest walks through, there is an increased expectation of profit. The larger the casino floor, the more games a person must pass, the more likely it is he will sit down and play. It's human nature.

Getting people to sit down is only half the battle. Once seated, the house must try to figure out how to keep you there as long as possible. There are free drinks so that no one has to get up to go to the bar (people also gamble much worse when they're drunk). Oxygen is pumped into the casino to give gamblers more stamina. There are no windows or clocks that might show evidence of the earth spinning on its axis, and the interior lighting is set perfectly so that when you catch yourself in the mirror, you look as healthy and robust as possible.

Every hotel-casino has its own strategy to lure players into its midst. Bugsy Siegel thought that the way to get people into his casino was to offer them luxury—the best food, the best shows—and even though it cost him his life, he was right. The Mirage Hotel has a fire-spewing volcano in front of its main entrance that erupts every fifteen minutes. Along the Vegas strip there are replicas of Venetian canals, the Eiffel Tower, the Empire State Building, and the Riviera of Monte Carlo. And all of that extravagant splendor is created to do one thing: get people into their joints. Once they are in there, human nature and the law of averages take care of themselves.

Benny Binion had a very different idea about gambling. His casino was originally designed with very few guest rooms, and they didn't have much in the way of comfort. The ceilings in his gambling hall were very low, the lighting was dim, and the only show you might see there was a cheater being cattle-prodded by security at the tables. Benny's thinking was very uncomplicated: "Good food cheap, good whiskey cheap, and good gamble. That's all there is to it."

While the other halls offered white tiger shows and drop-dead-gorgeous cocktail waitresses in short skirts, Binion offered what he called the "best gambling in town." He used to say that people got a lot of gamble for their money. Players who attended the opening of Binion's second casino, the Horseshoe, found things a little different there. Most casinos of the era had very low maximum-bet limits, perhaps $50 on craps and $150 on blackjack. That kept the customer at the table longer and meant the casino's risk was as minimal as possible. The more hands you participate in, the more often you bring the house edge into play, and therefore the more likely it is that you will lose. That's why there are table limits in place at all.

Low table limits contradicted everything Binion learned while running a game in Dallas. He knew that people who wanted to gamble wanted to gamble as high as they wanted. Binion set the table limit for craps at $500 and $200 for Keno, but decided that was too low. When Dave Berman—a partner of Bugsy Siegel in the Flamingo Hotel—found out that Binion was going to raise the Keno limit to $500, he threatened to kill him. The limits went up a few months later regardless.

When Binion started making his player-friendly changes, he forced other casino operators to get into the gambling business. With higher limits there was an element of risk on both sides of the game.

Binion's liberal rules aimed at pleasing the customer irritated Houssells, and because of it, their partnership broke down. In 1951 Binion set out on his own, opening the now legendary Binion's Casino on Freemont Street in downtown Las Vegas. In the 1960s he adopted a maximum bet policy; your first bet became your limit. This meant that anybody could bet any sum they wanted as long as they had the money to back it up. In 1980 a man named William Lee Bergstrom asked the Binion family if he could wager a million dollars on a game in their casino. Without a thought, Benny told the man that if he could get the money together, he could bet it.

A few months later Bergstrom walked into the casino carrying two huge suitcases. One was completely empty, the other contained $777,000. Ted Binion, Benny's son, was the casino operator working at that time. Ted approved the bet, and then watched Bergstrom walk over to a craps table and wager the entire sum on a woman's roll. He bet "don't pass" and, in three rolls, won $777,000 from the Binions. He packed the money into the empty suitcase and walked to his car with Ted as his escort.

Bergstrom was not through. Over the years he would make a number of huge bets ranging from $90,000 to $590,000 at the Horseshoe, winning them all. A few years after that, Bergstrom lost $1 million on one roll at Binion's place and was found dead three months later in a hotel on the Las Vegas strip. He had taken his own life.

Binion was also the first casino operator to consider using poker to promote gambling. This was a truly revolutionary idea because the house has very little stake in poker. There is no casino edge built into the game for the simple reason that the house is not involved in the action; poker pits player against player, not against the house. The only interest the casino has is charging time for play. Most casinos see poker as a waste of floor space, but Binion was different. He saw poker as yet another way to give the gambler what he wanted.

In 1949 a gambler named Nicholas Dandolos (a.k.a. Nick the Greek) approached Benny Binion with an odd request. He wanted to play the highest-stakes poker game ever played. The Greek had just come from the East Coast, where he reportedly had broken every gambler in New York and was said to be traveling with about $10 million. Binion took him very seriously.

There were already big poker games going on in back rooms all over Vegas. Bugsy Siegel (said to be one of the Greek's victims) had a $500,000 buy-in game in a room at the Flamingo. But what the Greek wanted was something completely different. He wanted to play in a game without limits, "heads-up," against only one opponent. That's why he came to Binion. Benny agreed to set up the game as long as the Greek was willing to play it in public. Binion thought it was a great way to get free publicity for his club.

The man Binion chose as the Greek's opponent was the legendary Johnny Moss, who was forty-two at the time. Moss, a friend of Binion's from the Dallas days, had also worked his way up from poverty by committing little scams and crimes. He admits to learning how to cheat at cards before he actually understood the rules of the games.

Binion flew Moss in from Dallas that day, and the game began later that night. All told, it would last for five months. The two opponents took time off only to sleep (although the Greek played craps most of the time when he was away from the table). The swings were huge. In the first two weeks of play Moss lost almost a million dollars to the Greek ($250,000 in one hand of five-card stud alone). He recovered and, in the end, broke the Greek, taking somewhere in the neighborhood of $2 million, and then he went to sleep.

Benny was right about the publicity the game would drum up. Day after day people would line up outside the casino to catch a glimpse of the action. Years later, in 1970, Binion decided to re-create the excitement and staged a poker championship tournament that he called "The World Series of Poker." That year the series was by invitation only, and the winner was chosen by a democratic vote of the players. After a week of playing they chose Johnny Moss as world champion.

The next year Binion changed the rules. What he created is now known as tournament gambling. The first thing he wanted to do was change the time the game took; those marathon five-month-long games were just too exhausting. Benny created a system in which the antes and blind bets would increase at certain predetermined times. Tight players who chose to bide their time, folding a lot, would eventually get anted and blinded to death. If you did not play aggressively, you'd find yourself with a penny-ante stack of chips in front of you while the game had progressed into a $1,000 buy-in stake.

The next thing Binion did was turn the game into what he called a "freeze-out." This meant that you were not allowed to leave the table until one of two things happened: You lost all of your money, or you won every chip on the table. Those were your two options. This exciting new format was a huge media hit. National television coverage of the tournament started in 1977.

The last change Binion made was to open the tournament to the public—and therein lay the magic. If you had $10,000 you were willing to gamble, you were more than welcome to sit down. Poker players around the country loved the idea of playing against the best in the world. Imagine being able to buy your way into suiting up for the Super Bowl. That's how the World Series became known as the cemetery of the hometown hero.

In the first year there were seven participants. The next there were thirteen. The third year there were twenty. In 1981, the tournament began to offer satellites. These were smaller tournaments with $200 buy-ins, and if you won that competition, you would win a seat at the big game. In 1982 the World Series drew 52 entrants; by 1999 the event attracted 3,456 entries. And the total prize money was a staggering $11,280,000.

There are now thousands of poker tournaments held around the world every year, with an estimated 75 million participants. Each one has copied some aspect of Benny Binion's tournament.

I only saw Benny Binion once in my life. It was the winter of my freshman year in college. One Friday afternoon my close friend Justin and I left Vassar with the intention of going to Atlantic City for the night. Somehow we got sidetracked and ended up on a plane that landed in Las Vegas at around midnight (maybe this is part of the reason it took me a little more than the standard four years to graduate from college).

We each had brought $200 to gamble with. The fact that we spent almost double that on the plane tickets didn't seem to bother us. Our intention was to make our little nest egg last as long as possible, so we decided to play very low-stakes poker until our plane departed early Sunday morning.

"Binion's is the only place to go," Justin told me.

"What's Binion's?" I asked.

Justin laughed. "What the hell kind of poker player are you?"

Forty-five minutes later, Justin and I were standing in the café of Binion's Casino when a very old man wearing a huge white cowboy hat ambled by us. Justin stopped him. "Are you Benny Binion?" he asked.

"I sure think so," Binion replied. "Where you boys staying tonight?"

"We haven't figured that one out yet," Justin told him.

"Well, go see Gus in reception. I'll tell him to give you two guys a room." And then he walked off.

Justin and I ran off, giddy from our encounter with Vegas royalty, and proceeded to drop every penny we had at the poker tables. We didn't really care; we were going to spend the rest of our weekend in our complimentary room getting drunk on complimentary booze. So we went to see Gus and told him our story.

"Benny told me you'd be coming by," Gus said. Justin and I exchanged a confident, worldly glance. "So," Gus asked, "how'd you like to pay for the room?"

"Pay for it?" I asked, outraged. "I thought he was giving us a room."

"That's not what he told me."

Completely broke, we spent most of the next thirty-six hours playing catch with a ball made out of rubber bands in the Vegas airport.

Well, it's still a pretty good story—though I have to admit, most of the time I tell it at a card table, I stop right before we lose all of our money.

Benny Binion died on Christmas Day, 1989.

I THINK THAT GUY IS FULL OF @*!#

Put yourself in their shoes before you decide on the best way to take their shirts.

—DAVID SKLANSY,
professional poker player and writer

In 1944 famed mathematician and Manhattan Project scientist John von Neumann wrote a book with Oskar Morgenstern titled *Theory of Games and Economic Behavior.* In it, they defined an area of mathematics called game theory. In short, game theory is a way to give mathematical explanations to real-life situations and competitions. In a chapter entirely devoted to poker, von Neumann created elaborate mathematical explanations for the actions governing the game. He assigned probability and monetary value to certain hands and concluded one thing: the game of poker cannot be played without bluffing.

In its most rudimentary form, poker is a game where one player says, I am willing to bet that my hand is better than yours.

It takes another player to doubt that, to assume that *his* hand is actually the best, for the game to continue. If you play the way that von Neumann assumed in his initial calculations—very mechanically, where the amount you are willing to wager increases proportionally with the strength of your hand—then as a player, you become extremely predictable. Other players would be able to accurately guess the strength of your hand as soon as you made a wager. The only time you would ever have a bet called (and possibly make more money than the ante) is when you actually hold the weaker hand, which makes for a really long night. That's why attributes like deceptiveness and savvy are so essential to the game. Sometimes you have to represent cards that you don't have, because if you don't, you might as well play with your hand faceup for everybody to see.

My friend Eli Angel comes to mind when I think of von Neumann's conclusion. Eli's last name fits him perfectly—he is about the nicest man I've ever met. To add to this image of angelicness, Eli bakes cookies for a living. I've been playing with him at my club for almost three years now, and my hand to God, I've never seen him turn over cards that he didn't represent. And I'm not the only person to notice this. He's well known for never, ever bluffing. It's like he thinks representing cards he doesn't have would be dishonest. And because of that, Eli gets very little action at the table. I'll never call a bet or raise his unless I have great cards. I suspect other people feel the same. Therefore, the pots he does win are never as big as they should be. What makes his situation worse is that he looks like a nice guy. He really does. So even if people didn't notice that he never bluffed, he just looks so sweet that people assume he's telling the truth. And that hurts you at a card table.

It helps to think of poker as two armies facing each other on a battlefield. If neither side is able or willing to deceive the other, then the outcome of the conflict can be concluded by simply counting heads. Wars used to be fought with that honorable etiquette. That's how the English kept conquering Scotland. They'd show up with an overwhelming number of troops and then negotiate a victory with the Scottish nobles. Now, this is a pretty good deal if you're some poor Highlander who just avoided being clubbed to death, but as a strategy of waging war, obviousness is a terrible tactic. When the possibility of deception is integrated into the formula, then you've really got something to work with.

On May 3, 1863, a Yankee brigade of some 1,600 men under the command of Colonel Abel Streight stood across a battlefield from a group of Confederate soldiers led by General Nathan B. Forrest. Exhausted from a long chase, the Yankees decided to dig in and wait for the fight. What they saw was unsettling. Wave after wave of Southern troops marched across a field and took up positions in the trees of a nearby forest. Scores of heavy artillery followed. By Colonel Streight's count, his Northern troops were outnumbered by at least 3 to 1, and they were probably outgunned by double those odds. Moments later the Yankee colonel agreed to lay down his arms and surrender.

A small band of Confederate soldiers entered the Yankee camp to collect weapons and organize the prisoners for the long march to an internment camp. When that was completed, and the signal was given, the rest of Forrest's men came out of hiding to escort the prisoners to Rome, Georgia. There were only six hundred men. What the Yankee brigade had actually witnessed was the same troops and heavy artillery marching in circles, out one side, across the battle line, into the forest, and then back out again. In actuality, Streight's forces had outnumbered the enemy by over a thousand men.

There is a perfect example of a well-thought-out bluff that was executed exquisitely. The player with the worse cards won the hand. Forrest's deception might not have ended there. Let's say, theoretically, the two commanders confronted each other a second time. Forrest marches his men into the trees again, and Streight thinks to himself, "You know what, I've seen this before, and there's no way I'm gonna get fooled again." So he orders his troops to charge. But this time Forrest actually does outnumber his opponent 3 to 1. Instead of retreating, as they should have, Streight's men get slaughtered.

Showing an ability to represent strength that you do not possess conjures in your opponent's head the most essential question in poker: Does he have what he claims to? That's why there's no such thing as an unsuccessful bluff. If it works, fantastic, you win the pot. If it doesn't, and after a huge raise you get called, and turn over your cards and proudly show your jack-high, then at least you've shown that you have the capacity to bluff. It's like an advertising budget.

My brother does that kind of thing very well. Unlike Eli, his appearance is an asset at a card table. He's got these huge hands. They're like two catcher's mitts, and when he plays poker, the cards kind of get lost in his grip. It's rather intimidating. You sit across the table from him, and you think that if you put a bad beat on him, he just might reach across the table and pull out your larynx. Whenever he bluffs, whether it works or not, he calls attention to it. I used to think he was just showing off by unnecessarily revealing his hand after winning with a bluff, but he wasn't. He was just making sure that everybody saw that, on occasion, he's willing to misrepresent his hand. Once he shows the ability to bluff and take a chance, he gets people doubting the strength of his cards on almost every occasion, even when he has the nuts. Therefore, he's got a lot of players calling his final bet just to see if he actually has what he claims. And that makes him a more profitable card player.

There are other ways to bluff than just acting strong when you are weak. Take the heavyweight championship title fight known as "The Rumble in the Jungle" as an example. In 1974 Muhammad Ali and George Foreman squared off against each other in Kinshasa, the capital of Zaire. The fight was thought to be a mismatch. Members of the media, Howard Cosell in particular, said that Ali was too old and too tired to put up even a respectable fight against Foreman. He was such a huge underdog (the official line was 4 to 1) that people were concerned not only for Ali's reputation but for his life as well.

The fight started out just like it was supposed to, with Foreman punishing Ali. The most unforgettable image of the contest was Ali being brutalized by the huge fighter, leaning back against the ropes like, to quote George Plimpton, "a man looking out his window to see if there was something on his roof."

Foreman saw the exhausted Ali floundering against the ropes and took the opportunity to go for the kill. He spent the seventh round of the bout throwing everything he had at Ali, and consequently punched himself into a state of total exhaustion. When Foreman's breathing became labored and his punches became weak, Ali fought his way off the ropes and went after Foreman with all that he had. Ali had been playing possum, bluffing that he had nothing left, and Foreman fell for it. To the surprise of everybody but himself, Ali dropped the undefeated champion in the next round.

Unlike General Forrest, who faked strength when he was weak, Ali did the opposite, feigning exhaustion when he was just getting ready to fight. This, in poker, is analogous to "slow playing." The most common form of this technique is the maneuver called a check-raise mentioned earlier. A player with a strong hand chooses not to place an opening bet and checks, acting as if he has weak cards, thereby luring his adversary into making a wager. Once this is done, and it is his turn to call, he surprises his opponent by making a raise instead.

The purpose of this bluff is to lull the opposing player into a false sense of security. Two possible scenarios can result from a check followed by a raise. Suppose your opponent has a weak hand. If you open with a bet instead of checking, he may well fold. You only win the ante. If you check, this might convince him that his cards aren't that bad after all, at least in relation to yours, so he bets, trying to steal the pot. Then instead of folding or even calling, you raise, in all probability he will fold. You win that extra bet he made because you played possum.

The second scenario holds if your opponent has good, but not great, cards. If you open with a bet, he's just going to call. But if you open by checking, and he likes his hand, he's going to bet, and then you can raise him. If he folds, the first scenario holds, but if he likes his hand enough, he'll call to see the next card. The pot is now much bigger than had you only won the ante.

Playing deceptively also serves another purpose. Check-raising is a way of warning your competition not to take advantage of apparent weakness. You are no longer the guy who plays obviously, the guy whose cards can be read without a thought. Checking is no longer a sign of absolute weakness. The next time you have a borderline hand and check, your opponent will be more reluctant to bet because of the chance that you may come back at him with a raise. He'll choose not to bet, and you'll end up seeing a lot of turn and river cards for free.

That's *why* you bluff; the question now becomes how *often* you should bluff. There are libraries full of instructional guides written by gamblers trying to answer that question. The fact of the matter is, there is no clear conclusion. You have to assess every situation individually.

The most important factor to consider in deciding when to bluff is who you are playing with. To win at different card tables, you have to employ different strategies. And even though this sounds counterintuitive, often the most productive strategy is to mimic your competition. If they are not particularly savvy, then play a very simple game. Bad players usually make more mistakes by calling when they should have folded, not the other way around. Therefore, bluffing them isn't going to be that effective. In over a thousand Tuesday nights playing with my college buddies, I think I have bluffed on two occasions. There's honestly no point to it. Somebody is always going to call you in that game. The biggest mistake inexperienced poker players make is thinking that the only way to make money at poker is to win more hands. They have not recognized that the best way to make money is by minimizing your losses by folding more frequently. Because of that, almost no pots are ever taken down without having to show your hand. If there ever comes a time in my Tuesday-night game when I bet and nobody calls me, then maybe I'll start to believe I can win by bluffing. But until then, what's the point?

If you're like most of the millions of people across the planet who play poker, your game is probably somewhere between my Tuesday-night group and the final table of the World Series of Poker. If the World Series is the pinnacle of the game, you might wonder how much bluffing goes on there. Again, there's no one answer, but there is a pretty good rule of thumb: The better your competition is, the more important it is for you to play deceptively.

Which leads to the question of *when* to bluff. Well, first you have to find a clear objective to bluffing. If you're a tight player and bluff about once a night, then you are simply trying to win that one particular pot. If you have a reputation for only betting premium cards, then a big bluff once a game should undoubtedly buy you that one extra hand per night.

If you're not a particularly tight player, if you're a "loose goose" or "kamikaze" and you like an action game with plenty of calculated risk, then your objective should be to break even by bluffing. Don't get me wrong, you are trying to make a profit, but if you don't, it's not a big deal. If you think that sounds absurd, consider von Neumann's conclusion: There is no such thing as an unsuccessful bluff. If you break even, if you win as many times as you get caught, you may not make money specifically by bluffing, but you will increase the number of players that call you when you have great cards. So when you catch a full house and somebody has two low pair, he will be much more likely to call your big bet because he knows you have a tendency to bluff. That's where you're going to make your money.

Once you have a set objective, you can start employing your strategy. A lot of players make a huge mistake by incorporating deception into their game plan as if it were a quota, and represent hands that they don't have at seemingly random moments, no matter who they are playing against or what the cards look like. This is about as dumb a thing as you can do at a poker table. There are good times to bluff, and times to absolutely avoid it.

Poker starts out as a competition for the ante. Previously, I said that having a good hand and winning just the ante is a tremendous letdown. But, if you do that once per round, you are basically playing in the game for free. Therefore, stealing antes by bluffing is a very profitable way to play. There are opportune times to do this. Bluffing with bad cards for the ante can really work in a shorthanded game. The fewer players involved in the pot, the more likely it is that you are going to scare them all away. Remember, *everybody* has to fold for your ruse to work. If your move worked on every player but one, then it didn't really work, did it? It also helps to be in late position. If you're the last bettor, you can see what's going on around you. If you raise or bet in an early position, who knows what the players behind you are going to do? But if a lot of people have checked or folded, then you know you're up against some weak hands, and a big bet from you is likely to scare them all off.

There are, however, games played without antes. Those games have something called a blind structure. Most Hold'em, particularly those games offered in casinos and clubs, is played this way. The person directly to the left of the dealer is known as the "little blind." That person is responsible for wagering half of the first bet. That means in a $1–$2 game, the little blind must wager fifty cents before he even gets to look at his hand. The person directly to his left is called "the big blind." He has to bet the full amount ($1). Then the action continues clockwise, each player in turn decides whether or not to call the big blind's $1 wager. So you can never see the flop for free. There is a mandatory bet to begin the game.

Every player after the big blind has to either call, raise, or fold. There is no way to check on the first round of betting. Stealing blinds is similar to stealing antes in the sense that position is very important. So, if you're the dealer (or the "button" in a casino game), and every player has folded except the blinds, then a raise, regardless of your cards, is often going to buy you the pot. You are, after all, playing against two completely random hands. There is one other thing to take into consideration, and that is whose blinds are you stealing. You want, obviously, to attack the weak players. You're much more likely to get away with your robbery if the players are timid or tight. Some people hate to have their blinds stolen. I'm one of them. If the button is going to raise me, he'd better have the cards, because I'm always going to come over the top and raise him back.

Most of the time, those situations are ideal for bluffing because the table has basically announced that they have bad hands by checking or folding, or in a game with blinds, they've bet on hands they haven't seen. But what about the situation when somebody has raised before you? Most of the time it pays to simply muck your cards unless they're great. But if you are lucky enough to have position (you act after he does) on a very loose player who likes to bluff a lot, you're in perfect position to rebluff. Just raise his raise, and when the cards come out, you bet. He's probably going to assume that you have better cards than he does and fold right away. If the person who raises before you is a tight player, however, that's a different story.

Let's say that you're in a game of $10–$20 Hold'em with seven people. The little blind puts up his $5, the big blind his $10, and then the hand is dealt. The player to the left of the big blind is said to be "under the gun." He is the first person who has to make a decision based on his cards whether or not to call the $10 bet. He folds. The next person raises. Now it's your turn. You look down at your cards, the A♠ 10♠. This is a very borderline hand to call a raise with. You are losing to any ace with a jack, queen, or king kicker. And the other three aces in the deck are your only three outs against any pocket pair of face cards. In short, very few hands that a tight player might be holding are weaker than what you're holding. The two things that you have in your favor are that your cards are of the same suit, and that you have position on him.

Most of the time, this situation calls for you to muck your hand, but if you decide to play, it's important to not just call his bet. You should bluff that your hand is stronger than it is by raising his raise. This is a great way to see how good his hand actually is. If he just calls your raise, then you could be in fine shape. But if he "caps" the betting (makes the third and usually final raise), then you should put your opponent on one of the three premium hands he could be holding (pair of aces, kings, or queens). At that point you have to hope to get lucky and draw to the flush, straight, or trip 10s.

Making the reraise is the most essential part of your play. Aside from setting up the bluff and gathering more information about his hand, you are scaring all the other players away. Most people will call a raise as the big blind because they are already committed to half of the bet (they have already wagered $10 of the $20, so they are getting a huge discount on participating in the hand). But they are going to be much more reluctant to call three bets because, obviously, you've made it more expensive for them.

Let's say that the rest of the players have folded, and you are heads-up with the original raiser. The success or failure of your bluff now depends on the flop. First, think about what a bad flop for you might be. If there is an ace and/or a king in the first three cards shown and your opponent comes out betting, that's a great time to cut your losses and toss your hand into the muck. Even if the ace flops, giving you the top pair with a decent kicker, and he bets, there is still a strong probability that you're holding the losing hand. If he has an ace and another face card, then you are essentially drawing to three outs (the other 10s) in the deck. You are a huge underdog, and there is not enough money in the pot to make chasing him worthwhile. If there is an ace on the flop, and he checks, then you can put him on something like pocket jacks and bet away with your pair of aces.

If the flop is three rags, say 3♠ 7♥ 9♣ , this is your time to bet.

Don't be alarmed if he calls. Most players holding an ace with another face card will match the first bet, as it's only $10, regardless of the flop. If the turn card does not pair him up, when you make a $20 bet, he's almost always going to fold his ace-king, even though he has the winning hand. And that's because he thinks you've got better. Your reraise of him preflop has implied a big pocket pair, and that is going to scare him to death. He's likely to muck his big slick to your ace-10, even though there was never a time in that hand when your cards were better than his.

Keep in mind that this does not mean you are going to win every pot that you reraise with ace-10. It's important to realize that even though you decided to bluff at the very beginning of the hand, there were three or four times during the play that you had to consider abandoning your plan. That's what bad players forget. They don't realize that there are really bad situations to bluff in.

Take, for example, a hand where you've raised with the 6♠ 8♠ and you got four callers. The flop comes K♥ J♥ 9♣ . This is a terrible situation to continue your bluff. Most average players will call with any two face cards in Hold'em. That said, somebody out there certainly has a pair, or maybe even two. It's likely there's a player who's drawing to a straight and possibly another person drawing to the flush. With those cards on the flop and four callers, it's time to abandon the bluff and muck your cards.

Beyond a total bluff where a player has little chance of actually winning the hand if he is called, there is something called a pseudo or semi-bluff. Take, for example, a game of Hold'em, where you are one-on-one with another player. You played $\boxed{J\diamond}\boxed{10\diamond}$. The flop is the $\boxed{9\clubsuit}\boxed{7\heartsuit}\boxed{2\diamond}$. You check because you didn't hit much of the flop. Then your opponent bets. If you suspect he's just making a position bet—trying to buy the pot because you represented a bad hand by checking—then you should call. You still have two over cards and an inside straight draw (known as a "gut shot") with an 8. The turn is the queen of diamonds. Again, this card did not hit you in the sense that it gave you a made hand, but now you have a huge draw. You have almost every out imaginable. There are nine cards that give you a flush (all the remaining diamonds), six cards (the 8s and kings that are not diamonds) that will give you a straight, and six cards (the remaining jacks and 10s) that would give you a decent pair. That's almost half the deck. This is a perfect situation for a semi-bluff. Instead of betting out, you check-raise him, which announces that you have a huge hand. If he was bluffing, he'll throw his hand away immediately. If he calls, you'll have to take your chances and see the hand through. If you hit one of your twenty-one good cards, then praise Jesus and hope he calls your bet. Let's say the other player had a king-9, giving him top pair with a great kicker after the flop, and the river is an ace, he will think twice about calling a bet on the river because he is going to assume, since you check-raised on the turn, that the queen hit you, or at least the ace on the river did, and if he's any good, he'll save the final bet by folding.

Semi-bluffs work even better if you have position on your opponent. If you played the K♥ 10♥ and the flop is Q♥ J♥ 4♣, then you have a four-straight flush. If your competition has a jack or a queen, you have two shots (turn and the river) at eighteen outs (nine hearts, three aces, three 9s and three kings), making you the favorite. Your opponent bets. You call. The turn card is the 6♦, which doesn't help you at all, and he bets. If you raise him, and he's got a small pocket pair or even an ace-king, there's a good chance he's going to fold even though he's winning. Who knows, if he's a catastrophist and has a jack, he might even assume you have a queen and lay down his hand. But the important part is that after you raised, he's unlikely to bet the river. In essence, you have paid the exact same amount (assuming he would have bet the river), but you have a better chance of winning, because he might lay down his hand.

Semi-bluffs also work very well in a game of five-card draw. If you are dealt a low two pair and are up against very few opponents, that's a great time to represent a much bigger hand than you are holding. You make the largest bet or raise as the game allows, and then, when the draw comes, you stand pat. Since your odds of drawing to the full house are 15 to 1 against, you take no cards and represent a made hand. Following the draw, bet the maximum, and any player holding low trips or a better two pair than yours is going to assume you were dealt a straight or a flush and muck their cards. Even if you get called, two pair is a decent enough hand to back up your bluff. If you lose to a straight, or three of a kind, your actions have assured that next time you *are* dealt a pat hand like a full house, there's going to be somebody who remembers your bluff who will call any bet and lose with their two pair.

Now the big question becomes, How do you decide if somebody is bluffing? Well, there are actually hundreds of ways to figure that out. They're called tells.

TELLS

A guy walks into a bar and notices three men and a dog playing poker. The dog is playing beautifully.

"That's a very smart dog," the man says.

"Not really," says one of the players. "Every time he gets a good hand he wags his tail."

My close friend Steve and I spent the last week of August 1984 up in the Adirondack Mountains at my grandmother's place. Even at an awkward sixteen, Steve had a fantastic gift for finding women to date, no matter where he was. He had a girlfriend at the time to whom he was supposed to be faithful, but for as long as I've known him, that sort of nominal monogamous commitment has been inconsequential. On this summer trip he managed to conjure up a female companion out of the limited population of Paul Smith, New York, and proceeded to spend most of his six-day vacation with her. The night we got home, Steve and I met some friends at a restaurant, one of them being his girlfriend. He walked up to the table and kissed her passionately. She looked him dead in the eye and said, "I can't believe you cheated on me again."

After the obligatory exchange of accusations and denials, Steve finally confessed to his infidelity and groveled for forgiveness. A few hours later she accepted his apology (wasn't high school great?) and they went on to another glorious three weeks of being together. After receiving absolution that night, Steve asked his girlfriend how she figured out his indiscretion so quickly.

"Easy," she said. "First, you didn't look at me while you were walking over to the table. You were staring at the ground the whole time. Second, you kissed me like you were some porn star. And to top it all off, once I accused you of cheating on me, all you did was smile and blink." I looked over at Steve while she was saying this, and sure enough, he was smiling and blinking like crazy. Steve had, as it's known in poker, a tell.

Pop psychologists theorize that tells are unintended actions birthed in the subconscious. At an early age most people are taught a number of rules meant to govern their actions throughout their lives. Parents and teachers, and even the Bible, preach to us that nothing bad can happen if we tell the truth. That rigorous education settles into the subconscious and becomes the foundation for the character we display as we grow into adults. Tells are simply a result of a conflict between the notion of morality implanted by authority figures during our childhoods and our intention to deceive.

We give our little secrets away every day, even though we don't want to. It's said that only the guilty sleep well in jail. The theory goes that if you're guilty and get caught, you figure that you are where you belong and might as well get some sleep. An innocent man tosses and turns, trying to figure out how to resolve his situation.

We are riddled with these tics and twitches. They are everywhere and in everything we do. Those of us who have not been trained to deceive have a tendency to cover our mouths or avoid eye contact when telling lies. That's why I've never dated an actress. While normal people are studying the market economy of the original thirteen colonies or trigonometry, actors are learning how to look you dead in the eye and issue an absolute fabrication.

Our innate desire to tell the truth is most counterproductive at a card table. Having a poker tell can be disastrous. When I was just learning the game, I bought a book called *The Body Language of Poker: Mike Caro's Book of Tells*. I actually never got around to reading it until the night after I got knocked out of the 2000 World Series. Caro described a tell in which a player, thinking about whether to call a bet, suddenly asks the dealer or another player how much it costs to raise. Caro's point was that anybody playing in a decent-size game knows how much it costs to bump a bet. Somebody taking a lot of time and then asking that question has got to be trying to seem stupid or desperate. When I read that, I thought, Caro's got to be making that one up. No one's that dumb.

The next day I went to watch the final table of the tournament I'd just gotten knocked out of. When I arrived, there were only three players left, all great talents. At one point Melissa Hayden bet into Men Nguyen—a three-time champion—and he just sat there looking confused. After a while Men looked at his cards and then asked an official how much it cost to raise. The guy told him, and then Men raised. Melissa called, and Men turned over a full house, laughing as he collected the pot. I guess even the great players have tells.

Overcoming a tell is as difficult as changing any habitual aspect of your personality. I knew a cardplayer who videotaped his regular card game every week for a year. He would watch the tapes for hours and take notes about his mannerisms and reactions to make sure that his body language wasn't giving away anything about his hand. He found that even after playing the game for thirty years, he still had, by his estimate, about ten noticeable tells.

I asked him if he thought that any of these were severe enough for other players to notice. Without a thought he said, "I don't know, you tell me. I smile when I have good cards and pout when I don't. Think somebody was gonna pick that one up eventually?" He had a good point there.

If you think about it logically, anyone playing poker is trying to deceive his opponents. It's essential to the game. Therefore, most tells become common sense. In Texas Hold'em, if somebody hits the flop huge, what is he going to do? Well, common sense dictates that since he is trying to deceive, he'll act as if the flop missed him completely. And sure enough, a lot of players do just that. It's a huge tell. They feign disinterest in the hand. They will look away, watch TV, talk to other players, anything but look directly at the cards on the table. Somebody who stares at the flop for a long time almost certainly missed it. It's like he is examining it in the hope that he will suddenly notice something new.

Now I'm going to do something extremely stupid. For the benefit of my readers, I am going to open up my book of tells that has taken me almost twenty years to create, and let everybody I've ever played with know what their little tic is. I suspect it's going to cost me in the long run, but hey, nothing is as important to me as the happiness of those who have taken the time to peruse this work.

I'll start with my brother. I mentioned before that he's a sturdy player. In fact, he's such a sturdy player that he remains completely calm when he's bluffing. His hands are steady as a rock when he's betting out with garbage. But, and this took me a long time to figure out, when he's got the nuts, and he's got a player trapped, he gets so excited that his hands shake. They tremble when he's got the winning hand.

There are some other classic tells in my Tuesday-night game. Johnny California, a man with the worst posture in the history of primates, sits up straight as a board when he's got good cards. Tom Lemme has a chip-stacking giveaway. When he bets and stacks the chips neatly while putting them in the pot, he usually expects to be getting the chips back. When he throws them into the pot aggressively, he's usually trying to pull off a bluff. And when he tosses them in sloppily, he's usually making a very reluctant call.

I feel like a heel admitting this, but the kind math professor who mentored me through my developmental years of poker in graduate school had a tell. I never told him that I picked it up. I guess I should have, but we used to play together a lot, and keeping it to myself saved me a lot of money. I know that's no excuse. My good friend the professor had a tendency to quickly look at his chips when he hit a good card. It was far from a casual glance. As soon as the good card came up, his eyes shot to his stack of chips. It's like he wanted to make sure that his money was still there to bet with. If, for example, we were playing Texas Hold'em and he had a pair of nines after the flop, and the turn card came up a nine, giving him three nines, he'd stare at his chips and then look away into the distance. I knew what that meant. I folded a lot of top pairs after the turn was dealt when he looked at his chips like that. Sorry, Doc. A better man would have told you sooner.

He is a perfect example why a player should never look at the flop as it's being dealt. Most people get so fixated on what cards are about to come that they often give something away by their reaction. Don't watch the cards while they are being dealt; watch the faces of the players watching the cards being dealt. You can check your hand later. It's not going anywhere. Just see if anybody flinches or blinks or smiles or even looks away when the flop hits the table. It'll certainly tell you something about what's going on around you. This is also the very reason why dealers flip all three cards in flop games at the same time. That way, nobody can clock a player's reaction to each individual card as it comes out.

There are two great tells in my big Monday-night Wall Street Hold'em game. Andrew Megget has this weird way of looking at his cards. He picks them up so only one card is visible, then puts them back down on the table, slides one over the other, and then lifts them again so he can see the second card. He does this the same way every time. Well, almost every time. Occasionally, Andrew takes a second look at the first card. It took me the better part of a year to figure out why this happened. When the first card is inconsequential, like a 5 of clubs, he quickly looks at the second. But if the second card is an ace, he's got to flip back to the first one to see if the suits match because he didn't pay much attention the first time. In every instance that he examined his cards a third time and then called the bet, he's played an ace and a small card of the same suit. Knowing this, of course, is a huge help.

The other great tell in that game is Chris Wigmore. He was, for a long time, a very conservative player; but sometime in the mid 1990s he took a job at an Internet company and made a fortune. Chris started playing very loose after cashing in on those stock options. He's now got a very aggressive game. But even though his checkbook has allowed him to be so carefree at the table that it seems like money means nothing to him, his subconscious is stuck back in 1991, when he was a lowly ad exec, hoping not to lose so much in a $5–$10 game that he couldn't pay his rent. Whenever he makes a big bet in my direction, I just kind of sit there and wait. He probably thinks that I'm calculating pot odds or something like that, but I'm not. I'm just waiting for him to get uncomfortable. When he's got a great hand, Chris is dead serious. He waits me out without saying a word. When he's bluffing, he *tries* to act like he's waiting me out, and strikes up nonchalant conversations with people at the table. That's when I call him.

Chris also has a funny tendency to separate his winnings from his buy-in. This doesn't make much difference in limit games, but in no-limit, that can be a huge disadvantage. A player who stacks his chips this way is obviously very concerned with his outcome. He likes to know that he's up. So whenever we're playing no-limit, if Chris has the $300 stacked separately from his two grand buy-in, I know that—unless he's got a huge hand—any raise over that $300 will usually knock him out, because he wouldn't want to end with less money than he started with.

While I was at Wesleyan I used to play with a guy we called Stoner. He was, as his nickname implies, a full-on dope fiend. Stoner was peppered with practical tells. It's not that he wasn't smart enough to figure them out and make corrections, it's just that he didn't really care enough to change. If the flop was three cards of the same suit, and Stoner didn't look at his pocket cards and did bet, I always knew he had a flush. But if after a suited flop he looked at his pocket cards right away, then I knew he was too high to remember what suits they were and had to check them before figuring out what to do. If, after checking his cards, he called any bets, then I knew he didn't have the flush yet, but one of his pocket cards definitely matched the suit on the board, and therefore he needed one of the two cards left to make the flush. He'd do the same thing in seven-card stud. If he got his third of one suit on fifth street and had to pick up his down cards to check them out, then I knew that he didn't have the flush just yet.

Stoner also was one of those players that never bet an incomplete hand in five-card draw. If he was dealt a four flush or straight, he always checked or called and then drew one card. But if he bet or raised and then took one card, that meant he had two pair. Also, the way he looked at the drawn card was always a huge giveaway. When he was on a flush draw, he'd shuffle the drawn card into his hand and then squeeze it out slowly.

He'd do the same thing in seven-card stud. When he was dealt the river card, if he shuffled it into the rest of his down cards, then he was always on a draw. If he just picked it up and looked at it, then he always had a made hand before the river.

The last hand Stoner and I ever played together was a heads-up game of pot-limit five-card draw. He dealt me the A♥ K♥ 3♠ 8♠ 9♣ . I had been losing all day, so I opened the betting with $3. Stoner called. I threw the 3, 8, and 9 away and drew three cards. He drew one. After dealing himself the card, he picked it up and looked at it. I miraculously drew a 10, jack, and a queen, ended up making an ace-high straight (known as "Broadway"), and bet the maximum. He raised me back the amount of the pot. That was a scary raise. Against any other player I would have been terrified that they had made a full house or a flush. But not Stoner. Since he had just called my original bet, and then taken one card, I knew he didn't have two pair, so a full house was out of the question. And then after he dealt himself the one card, he picked it up and looked at it—he didn't shuffle it into his hand and squeeze it out like he does when he's looking for a flush. So I knew he had a straight. Since I had the highest straight possible, the worst I could do was chop the pot with him, so I raised him back the value of the pot. We each raised once more, then he finally called and flipped over his king-high straight. He lost over $200 in one hand of a heads-up game with a dollar ante. And that's hard to do.

He actually accused me of cheating after that hand because my last raise was, in his eyes, suspicious. He wanted to know how I didn't put him on a flush or a full house and therefore just call him. Well, buddy, here's your answer.

That hand that I played with Stoner was a perfect example of the deductive reasoning necessary to becoming a winning poker player. Each observation alone didn't help me all that much. But when I put them all together, it became extremely useful information.

Obviously, the more familiar you are with a player, the longer you play against them, the easier they are to read. Over time, you make notes about their play, and eventually you will be able to predict their actions. There are, however, certain universal truths about human nature that translate directly to the card table. Take any cliché about the human psyche, and you will find something that applies to poker players.

Somebody much smarter than me once said, "The vigor of youth gives birth to the misconceptions of immortality." It's a little flowery for my taste, but has a fantastic application at the poker table. Younger players have not yet become jaded by years of improbable beats. They feel virile at a table. For the most part, the younger the player, the looser they are, and the more likely it is that they will bluff. Older players tend to be wiser, more in control of their emotions, and play a much more straight-up game. The older a player is, the less likely it is that he will represent cards that he doesn't have.

The things players do and say unrelated to poker often open a revealing window into their psyche. Drunks bluff more. People betting on sports or the horse races while playing poker only participate in hands when they have premium cards because their attention is being diverted elsewhere and they're not concentrating enough to bluff with any savvy. Same is true for people eating at the table. Individuals who dress up for the game in fedora hats or fancy sunglasses often play a complicated game. They'll bluff or semi-bluff and slow play a lot more than the average player.

A few nights after I got knocked out of last year's World Series, I played a medium-size pot-limit Texas Hold'em game at Binion's. There was one hand in which I found myself heads-up with a gentleman who looked exactly like Uncle Fester from the Addams family. After many raises and reraises, the river was dealt. By the last card I had exactly what I started with, a pair of jacks. There was no possible flush on the board, no easily playable straight, and the only card that was higher than my jacks was a queen that came on the river. I had ended each round of betting before the river, meaning that I had either bet or raised and Fester had called me. But as soon as the river was dealt, Fester bet the pot—about $500. Now, I had never met this man before in my whole life. I had no real thought about him before that hand other than to picture him with a lightbulb in his mouth. I had no way to figure out whether he was bluffing or not. I decided to try an old standby move; I faked like I was going to call his bet by motioning toward my chips while watching to see if he had any reaction to my move. Most of the time a player will react to a called bet. If he slumps in his chair, he's got nothing. If he jumps toward his cards to flip them over, he usually has a huge hand. Well, Fester didn't do anything. He just sat and watched me. He did, however, get steamed that I tried such a sophomoric move on him. So he started to coffeehouse me. "What the hell was that, you trying to steal the money, kid? What you gonna do with it anyway, buy some Rogaine?"

I had managed to piss off a total stranger, which I didn't feel so good about. But then I began to think about his insult. Now, I do have a receding hairline, that is an undeniable fact, but I still have a good deal of hair on my head. So what was this gentleman trying to say? If some guy with a full head of Fabio hair levied that volley at me, I would have thought that he was trying to piss me off and therefore make me call with a losing hand, so I'd fold. But this man was full-blown, Telly Savalas bald. I'm not even sure he had eyebrows. Some guys can get away with that sort of look, but it wasn't particularly flattering on him. So what's up with the pot calling the kettle puce? Why is he talking to me about Rogaine? I saw it for the desperate insult it was, so I called. Fester turned over his pocket tens, I turned over my jacks, and the dealer pushed me the $1,000 pot.

My read on Fester could have been completely wrong. He could have predicted my reasoning and insulted me, hoping that I'd call. That's why a lot of players actually have fake tells. They are, after all, trying to deceive you. But one thing is certain—the more you pay attention to the body language of your opponents, the less money you'll leave on the table when you walk away.

WANT TO BET ON IT?

> *Man, Gamblers Anonymous must be desperate*
> *for new members. I just read their twenty questions*
> *to see if you're a compulsive gambler,*
> *and they make it too easy to qualify.*

—KOREAN RICH,
poker player

Early in the spring of 1999, Sal the Bookie, affectionately known as "Sally Books," was scheduled to be released from the Rikers Island penitentiary where he was completing an eighteen-month sentence for the promotion of gambling. Two welcome-home parties were simultaneously planned. The first was to take place at his house on Manhattan's Upper East Side. There, Sal's wife of ten years had been busy preparing for his release all week. She had cleaned the house meticulously, cooked his favorite meal, and invited over a few family members for a small dinner. Their three children, who had not seen Sal once during his year-and-a-half incarceration, had been bathed, brushed, and groomed within an inch of their lives and were instructed to be on their best behavior.

About four miles downtown another party was being planned. This one was at the Winchester Poker Club on Cortlandt Street in New York City. The owners of the establishment—all old friends and business acquaintances of Sal's—had put together an impressive spread for his return. There was pizza, a nine-foot submarine sandwich made with imported Italian cold cuts, refreshments and an elaborate dessert buffet. It created a festive mood in the club that night.

Most of the people there had never met Sal, or even heard of him for that matter. Their high spirits were due more to the complimentary food and drinks than anything else. Gamblers love free stuff. It's a universal truth. Doesn't matter what is being given away or what the reason is—some guy could drop $300 at a blackjack table, and on his way out, a casino host could put a hat on his head with the name of the casino that just took his money embroidered on it, and he'd suddenly feel fantastic about what had just transpired. It's a psychological abnormality essential to functioning as a gambler.

The evening of Sal's party I remember watching a man, easily $4,000 in the hole from a game of stud, line up at the buffet, giddy and wide-eyed like a kid on Christmas morning because he was about to get a complimentary slice of pizza. He didn't seem to care that he was essentially spending about $500 per pepperoni.

Most of the conversations across the poker table that night were about Sal. People were wondering what he was going to do on his first night of freedom. Even though there were two parties being thrown for him, no one knew what his first stop would be. It was a given, said those who knew him best, that his first stop would be the uptown brothel that his brother had an interest in. The evidence for this conclusion was that Sal had specifically asked his wife not to pick him up at Rikers.

All of the bookmakers and shylocks in residence that evening thought Sally would definitely come to the club straight from the brothel. After all, many patrons of the Winchester owed Sally money, and he would want to collect some of his debts so he could see his family with more than the $45 bus fare that the city gives you when you leave prison in his pocket.

The patrons of the club who had themselves done some time in prison held a very different opinion. They were willing to give Sal the benefit of the doubt. Amir, a fifty-three-year-old video store owner with two stints at Rikers on his résumé, had his own thoughts on Sal's pending activities. "Sally just spent eighteen months surrounded by guys with nothing better to do than play cards. You think he's gonna come here and do the same thing? No fucking way. One hooker, two cannolis, and a couple of pats on the head for each of his kids. That's it. Three to one he's in bed with his wife by ten."

"I'll take that bet," said a poker player sitting across the table from Amir.

And then it happened. A chart was drawn on a poster-size piece of cardboard. Columns were labeled with times and places, and odds were set. Action was placed all over the board before the chart was even finished being drawn. The proposition of home vs. the club was set at 50–50. Arriving at the Winchester before midnight regardless of where he had been prior was a 2 to 5 endeavor (meaning that for every $50 wagered, you would receive a $20 profit). The longest odds on the board were for something they called a Force Majuere, which was spelled incorrectly. It was a 20–1 bet that some act of God (flat tire, hurricane, car bomb) would keep Sal away from home, the club, or the whorehouse past midnight. Knowing what I did about Sal, his brother, his kids, and his wife—which was absolutely nothing—I bet on the "Force Majuere," as it offered the best odds on the board.

Inherent in the act of gambling is the ability of the participant to perpetually omit the notion of natural truth. Once that is done, a person is able to look beyond the practical applications of math and reason and achieve a consciousness that resides in the place where statistics hold less relevance than rabbit's feet. And then, when the gambler has no choice but to be immersed in reality—when he loses, as almost all gamblers do, and has to pay up—then he must be able to dismiss the entire experience from memory. If he pawned his television the day before, he has to be able to act as if he never owned one. That way he can get out of bed and do the whole thing over again. The irony that we were taking time off from a poker game to wager on the whereabouts of a convicted bookie seemed to escape everybody.

By 10:00 P.M. Sal had not arrived at the Winchester yet. The odds of him showing at all at that point had dropped to 3 to 1. At midnight a voice came over the club PA system announcing that the party for Sally was going to be postponed for three to six months.

Apparently, just hours before his release, Sal had been caught placing bets with another shylock on the prison phones and subsequently had all his good-behavior time revoked. So that was the end of the party. All bets were voided at that point except one. No one could figure out whether or not being rearrested in prison constituted a force majeure. We began to wonder, was his continued incarceration an act of God?

Every prison has its own architectural identity. The newer ones are sleek, cold, efficient, and sterile. The older ones, like Rikers, look like huge, haunted houses encircled by razor-wire-topped brick walls.

The Baltimore County Correctional Facility—where I spent a bit of time in the early 1990s*—looked like a hybrid bomb shel-

---

*Please see appendix A for further explanation.

ter / public school. With its low ceilings and yellow cement walls that led in every direction, its interior seemed to have been designed to inspire teduim. There were signs everywhere—instructions on where to stand, directions to different parts of the jail, and reminders to the prisoners about every conceivable subject.

Baltimore County Correctional had a wall of public phones near the dining hall where inmates were allowed to make calls to lawyers or family members during certain hours if they had not had the privilege revoked. Above the phones was a giant sign, roughly two feet by ten feet, that in huge black type read,

EVERY OUTGOING AND INCOMING PHONE CALL
IS BEING TAPED

When I first saw the sign, I suggested to a guard that they would probably profit more from eavesdropping if that sign wasn't there. He agreed, but pointed out that the warning was present for legal reasons. "It's against the law to secretly tape your conversations. That sign is above every public phone in every joint across America."

When I heard that Sal had been busted making bets on the phone, I thought about what that guard had told me. Here was a man, incarcerated for almost a year and a half, so thrilled about getting out of prison, so juiced up about getting back to his regular life, that on the day he was to be released, he walked up to a phone situated below a sign that said his conversation was being taped and placed a bet on a football game. Clearly this man had a problem. His actions seemed way beyond his control. The way I saw it, what happened to Sally Books was an act of God. And I wanted to collect on my 20-1 on the force majeure.

Most people have some twitch: jellybeans, fancy coffee, booze, dope, bad movies, coconut, young boys or girls, it could be anything. Some obsessions are more offensive and destructive than others. Gambling is a tricky addiction, because of its subtleties. Most longtime alcoholics and smack addicts abuse their bodies to the point of physical deformation. Veins collapse, stomachs bloat, jaundice sets in, and it becomes apparent to the population at large what a bad place that addict is in. Although less physically taxing, gambling is perhaps a more sinister compulsion in the sense that it's easier to keep secret. There are no track marks for all the world to see. Gamblers' lives can be on the brink of collapse while they continue to project an air of normalcy until the very last second.

Money is different to compulsive gamblers than it is to the rest of the world. Most normal people see money as a way to buy things. Two hundred dollars looks like a family dinner or a couple of pairs of shoes. Four grand is a car. Even to junkies money has a tangible manifestation. Ten dollars is a dime bag. But to gamblers, money just translates into the means to gamble more; a way to perpetuate their addiction. And for that reason, it simultaneously has no value and all the worth in the world.

Consider the scene in Milos Forman's *One Flew over the Cuckoo's Nest*. Jack Nicholson is playing poker with some other inmates. They are using cigarettes for chips. Each smoke is worth ten cents. Danny DeVito's character, Martini, keeps breaking them in half and saying, "I bet five cents." Like a compulsive gambler, he can't seem to understand that the objects they are betting with have some other tangible use other than to be wagered. In breaking the cigarette in half, he takes something that has a value in society because it serves a purpose (to be smoked), and destroys it. Once it can't be smoked, it is worthless to others. Martini doesn't see that. He misses the point that the cigarette's value derives from its ability to be smoked, not to be gambled. He thought that as long as he could bet it, it retained its monetary representation. Jack Nicholson kept saying, "This isn't five cents, Martini, this is shit."

Lots of addicts talk about their vice as a vehicle to alleviate the pressures of everyday life—a solution to their problems. This is where the defining line of addiction becomes hazy. Is there a healthy way to employ vices as distractions or medicinal relaxation techniques? Or is everybody who has a drink at the end of the day an alcoholic?

I used to play poker because I had a tough time holding down a real job and I wanted to have something to do during the day and maybe make a little money. Then I found that I enjoyed myself while playing. I liked the people, I like the action, so after I finally found employment that suited my commitment deficiencies, I began to play for fun. I realized that after a session—win or lose—usually I had recovered from whatever was bothering me. Even immediately after my mother succumbed to cancer, when I was deeply depressed, failing out of graduate school, and playing poker about forty hours a week, I saw my time at the tables as therapeutic. There I was always calm and thoughtful—and social, distracted from the difficulties in my life. In those years, a poker table was where I was happiest.

One of the most important decisions in the history of humanity was reached after many hours of detached contemplation over a pot-limit poker game. Having been in office only a few months, President Harry S. Truman was faced with the grim reality of trying to find a humane and efficient way to end the hostilities of World War II. Victory over Japan was almost assured, but the pride and tenacity of the remaining imperial Japanese forces created an untenable situation in the Pacific theater. Truman's intention was to bring the war to completion with a minimum loss of life and without involving the Red Army in the Pacific.

The American trump card to this end was the product of the

highly secretive Manhattan Project: the atomic bomb. The implications of this application of the bomb—the enigma of the radioactive aftermath and its impact on the entire planet, and the loss of life on such a grand scale—troubled the American president to the point that he could not decide if such a destructive weapon could be used in the name of peace. He knew that his decision, regardless of what it was, would change the course of history and define his presidency.

Seeking solace after the Big Three meeting with Churchill and Stalin in Potsdam, Truman took a few days to relax at sea. It was there he planned to make his decision. From the moment he got on board, President Truman engaged in an almost continuos game of pot-limit poker with members of the press corps.

Those games were a fantastic way for him to escape. I've been there before. I'm sure we all have. Everybody at some point in life has felt like he had the weight of the world on his shoulders. But in Truman's case, he really did. Sure, he was using poker as a distraction in the days before an atomic bomb leveled the city of Hiroshima. But that in no way implies that he was reckless or irresponsible in the manner that he went about making his decision. He was simply trying to unravel the intricate repercussions of his pending actions, and he wanted time away from his advisers to come to his own conclusion.

Harry Truman was not a compulsive gambler. But how then is

that term defined? There is an organization dedicated to answering that question, Gamblers Anonymous, an offshoot of the wildly popular twelve-step program Alcoholics Anonymous. There are roughly 2,000 GA meetings that provide various services and support to nearly 35,000 troubled gamblers across the planet.

GA has something they call "the twenty questions," a method of self-diagnosis gamblers can use to see if they are in danger of becoming compulsive. The questions are:

1. Did you ever lose time from work or school due to gambling?
2. Has gambling ever made your home life unhappy?
3. Did gambling affect your reputation?
4. Have you ever felt remorse after gambling?
5. Did you ever gamble to get money with which to pay debts or otherwise solve financial difficulties?
6. Did gambling cause a decrease in your ambition or efficiency?
7. After losing did you feel you must return as soon as possible and win back your losses?
8. After a win did you have a strong urge to return and win more?
9. Did you often gamble until your last dollar was gone?
10. Did you ever borrow to finance your gambling?
11. Have you ever sold anything to finance gambling?

12. Were you reluctant to use "gambling money" for normal expenditures?

13. Did gambling make you careless of the welfare of yourself or your family?

14. Did you ever gamble longer than you had planned?

15. Have you ever gambled to escape worry or trouble?

16. Have you ever committed, or considered committing, an illegal act to finance gambling?

17. Did gambling cause you to have difficulty in sleeping?

18. Do arguments, disappointments, or frustrations create within you an urge to gamble?

19. Did you ever have an urge to celebrate any good fortune by a few hours of gambling?

20. Have you ever considered self-destruction or suicide as a result of your gambling?

The GA party line is that anyone surpassing seven positive responses has a problem. Truman probably would have replied yes to two (14 and 15). Sally Books, on the other hand, was probably a twenty for twenty. I checked five when I first asked myself those questions, though I'll keep which ones to myself.

One of the great contradictions of poker is that most players don't see what they do as gambling. They rationalize their trade by the fact that there is no inherent disadvantage to playing, as there is in all other casino games. In that way, poker is perhaps the most insidious of all gambling pursuits. Only idiots think that they can make a living by playing blackjack or throwing dice. You have to be an absolute fool to think that you're going to defy the odds and win against the house in the long run. But poker is seductive to compulsive gamblers because they think their skill has not only leveled the playing field, but given them an advantage. And in some cases that is true, but to play premium poker, and succeed, one must be patient, practical, and unemotional during the game—all characteristics that are absent from a compulsive personality.

When poker began to spread across the country in the mid-1800s, it met overwhelming opposition. Preachers used to hold town hall meetings and deliver Sunday sermons on the evils of poker. The cards themselves became known as the "devil's picture gallery," and frequent participants were seen as heretics.

In one of the first poker books ever written, *The Complete Poker Player* (1855), John Blackbridge constructed a poker blueprint for upstanding gentleman cardplayers. He assigned a number—$3,000 a year—as the limit for what a player could lose in a year and still remain respectable. He called it an "amusement fund." If you exceeded Blackbridge's number, you were then in danger of entering what he called "the depths of compulsion."

Plenty of individuals exceed their amusement fund playing poker. A young man known as Korean Rich (later referred to as Crazy Rich) started playing in New York card houses in late 1998.

A bright twenty-nine-year-old investment banker from some Ivy League school, Rich was introduced to the clubs a few months after his wedding by his new brother-in-law. At the beginning it was strictly a distraction, a way to get out of the house and blow off a little steam after a long day at the bank where Rich had been employed since getting his JD-MBA in 1995.

Rich was an anomaly at the club from the start, a nice-looking, well-spoken young man in a jacket and tie, treading water in a sea of sweat suits and polyester. Other players were fascinated by him, asking questions like, "So you go to work every day? I mean, *every* day?" And when he would say that he did, they would all laugh nervously, as if in the presence of a convict serving a life term.

Rich was a pleasure to play with. Most of all, he was a determined bather, a trait not always prevalent among poker players. The nature of the game is antithetical to hygiene. Six hours at a table, smoking, drinking coffee, crimping (sweating even though you're not hot) when you get good cards or take a beat—a lot of players just don't smell so good. But the reason people *really* loved to play with Korean Rich was because he was a huge fish.

The greatest contradiction about Rich's bad play was that he was probably the brightest individual in the room. He could calculate odds and outs faster than anybody. The man even possessed a decent card sense. Where his attributes fell short was in the area of self-control. He did not have an ounce of it.

What made him go from Korean Rich to Crazy Rich was that he was born to be a compulsive gambler. By some genetic quirk, Rich had this ungerminated seed of sickness in his DNA. He had managed to live twenty-nine years without finding out that he had an insidious gambling problem, but the moment he got cards in his hands, it was as if he finally figured out what he had been missing his whole life.

Someone once said that the person who invented gambling was smart, but the person who invented chips was a genius. If gamblers had to count out ten hundred-dollar bills every time they lost $1,000, a lot less money would be wagered. But the chips are meaningless. They are more like Lego blocks than money. When you lose a $200 pot, that's barely twenty chips. You hardly notice them gone from your stack. And at the end of your game, if you've lost all your money, you don't have to pay a thing. You've already cashed in. So all you have to do is walk away from the table. And Rich walked away a lot.

Rich was the man who coined the phrase, "I'd bet my liver to see the river." He was never going to fold his hand until there was absolutely no hope of winning—and even then he might call you just to see what you had. The biggest difference between serious poker and the kiddie-pool games that we all grew up playing is how many hands a person participates in. It's not uncommon in a game of college buddies or work pals to have every player call the opening raise. It is almost considered polite. But in a casino game of Hold'em or seven stud with ten players, four callers is thought to be a crowded pot. The reason for this is kind of obvious; statistically, most hands are not playable.

Take Texas Hold'em, for example. If you ranked all the possible starting hands by efficacy and earning power from A♠ A♥ down to 2♦ 7♣ (2-7 off suit is worse than something like 2-3 because there is no two-card straight possibility), you'd find that very few hands are worth playing. Below is a ranking of the most advantageous Hold'em hands.

Rank of efficacy	Hand	% chance of getting this hand or a more effective one	Odds of getting this hand or a more effective one
1	AA	0.45	220–1
2	KK	0.9	110–1
3	QQ	1.36	73–1
4	JJ	1.81	54–1
5	AK suited	2.11	46–1
6	TT	2.56	38–1
7	AK	3.02	32–1
8	AQ suited	3.77	26–1
9	KQ suited	4.07	24–1
10	AJ suited	4.37	22–1
11	AT suited	4.68	20–1
12	AQ	5.58	17–1
13	99	6.03	16–1
14	KJ suited	6.33	15–1
15	KQ	7.24	13–1
16	KT suited	7.54	12–1
17	A9 suited	7.84	11–1
18	AJ	8.75	10–1
19	88	9.2	9.9–1
20	QJ suited	9.5	9.5–1

Rank of efficacy	Hand	% chance of getting this hand or a more effective one	Odds of getting this hand or a more effective one
21	KJ	10.41	8.6–1
22	A8 suited	10.71	8.3–1
23	AT	11.61	7.6–1
24	QT suited	11.92	7.4–1
25	K9 suited	12.22	7.2–1
26	JT suited	12.52	6.9–1
27	A5 suited	12.82	6.8–1
28	A4 suited	13.12	6.6–1
29	QJ	14.03	6.1–1
30	A7 suited	14.33	5.9–1
31	K8 suited	14.63	5.8–1
32	KT	15.54	5.4–1
33	Q9 suited	15.84	5.3–1
34	A3 suited	16.14	5.2–1
35	A6 suited	16.44	5.1–1
36	A2 suited	16.74	5.0–1
37	QT	17.65	4.7–1
38	K7 suited	17.95	4.6–1
39	77	18.4	4.4–1
40	J9 suited	18.7	4.3–1

Note: When it says, "Odds of getting this hand or a more effective one," in the case of AA, there is no more effective hand. So that number simply represents the odds of being dealt AA. But for KK, the number represents the odds of being dealt AA *or* KK (AA is considered more effective than KK). So, for KT (the 32-ranked hand), that number represents the odds of being dealt any one of the hands listed above it.

What the table illustrates is that the odds of getting dealt a premium hand are about 20 to 1, and 4 to 1 against even receiving a playable hand (and J-9 suited is not very playable in most situations).

The saddest thing is that Rich knew this information. And yet no matter what hand he was dealt—forget J-9 suited, try something like 9-3 off suit—Rich was in. In Texas Hold'em any two cards can win, and Rich was out to prove it. It didn't matter if there was a raise or two or if the betting was capped, he called no matter what he had. He couldn't stand to miss any of the action.

It's not uncommon to see a player who employs this type of compulsive strategy go on a tear, his 9-3 making some ridiculous straight or two pair. For a little while, the poker gods will smile on him as he starts crushing premium hands one after another. But the law of averages always catches up to those players eventually. That's what it's there for. And as the chips dwindle, the greater the compulsion to play becomes.

Rich's once-a-week sessions started to cost him big. He was losing about $500, a night. Third-year associates at the big New York City firms make in excess of a hundred and thirty grand a year, so at first his "amusement fund" looked like the better part of 30 g's a year. That's a brutal beating, but wasn't going to kill him.

His losing began to become unbearable when Rich started to go on twenty-four-hour-a-day tilt. His sessions at the club got longer and longer. He would play from six P.M. to five the next morning, go home, shower, tell his wife that he had been at the office late, and then head off to work. He'd pass out in his office, flake on two or three important meetings, go to the club, pass out again in the middle of hands, and then start the same miserable process over again. He was like some Laurel and Hardy routine. "I lost all my money . . . so I have to play poker to make it back . . .

but then I lost more money . . . so I had to play more."

When the firm first suspended Rich and gave him a week to sort out whatever problem he was lying to them about, instead of seeing it as an awful turn of events, he rationalized his situation as his great opportunity to get even and then get out. Once a compulsive player is stuck, all he wants to do is get even. But once he's even, he's not stuck anymore, and where the hell is the impetus to quit at that point? So Rich borrowed every dollar he could, sold some stock, told his wife some lie, and took the bus down to AC.

He started playing $50–$100 Hold'em with a group of professionals, and being Crazy Rich, he went on a tear. Rich was running so well that he moved to the $200–$400 table. At the end of his first day he was up maybe twenty grand. He had gotten even. Rich could have gone back to his life at that point, but he chose to keep playing to have something to show for all his troubles.

When Rich sat down at the big table at the Taj Mahal the next day, the players were waiting. Every pro within one hundred miles had been called. Partner teams had driven all night to take his money. And they did. He drove home that night absolutely broke. He was fired from his job two weeks after returning to New York. His wife filed for divorce shortly after she found out that he had sold his wedding ring in Atlantic City.

A few months after Rich left town, a call came into the Winchester Club. It was from a woman who had had the misfortune to employ Rich as her money manager and have the same last name as him (a very common Korean name). She wanted to know what the Winchester Club was. When the owner who had fielded the phone call asked why she was inquiring, she told him that two $10,000 checks that she had given to Richard to invest had come back to her endorsed to the Winchester. The club owner then recalled that Rich financed his last trip to Atlantic City by endorsing two $10,000 checks from his "sister" over to the club. Turns out Rich was an only child. The Winchester Club repaid the woman, and Rich is still a wanted fugitive in the state of New York.

Hordes of experts think that compulsive gamblers lose their money under the delusional belief that the law of averages does not apply to them. They think that they will somehow transcend reality. In my experience—and this is particularly true for Korean Rich—most compulsive gamblers aren't delusional. I think they self-destruct intentionally. They play games they are historically unsuccessful at to punish themselves, as if they believe they are not worthy of the decent things they have created in their lives. There could be a million reasons. Pick your cliché—abusive parents, bad skin as an adolescent, it could be anything. I don't know enough about Rich to identify the genesis of his twitch, but he was certainly intent on ending up as he did: a wanted man.

TAKING IT LIKE A MAN

Gambling: The sure way of getting nothing for something.

—WILSON MIZNER (1876–1933),
con man and promoter

One of the biggest reasons losing less is more difficult than winning more is that losing begets losing. If you start with $500 and lose 50 percent, you've got $250 left. Now you've got to make 100 percent on your money to get even. Doesn't seem fair, right? Anybody can sit down, win a few hands, make some money, and then play like a champion. But playing from behind while you're down, keeping a cool head after an improbable beat, now that's really hard to do.

Second-best hands are often the reason players go broke. The impact of coming in second place in a poker hand is more far-reaching than just the standard irritation generated by parting with money. That kind of loss affects the mind in subtle ways. It causes doubt and apprehension to seep into your play. A bad beat will often ignite depressing thoughts such as, I should have paid my rent instead of giving these idiots my money. Frustration builds. Anger snowballs. And you lose more.

To quote my girlfriend, Tessa, after her first down session, "Losing sucks." This may be true, but regardless, it is an integral part of the game. Even the great players walk away defeated sometimes. In fact, they lose more often than you would suspect. They just do it in a more efficient manner than the rest of the poker population. That's part of the reason they are so successful. As a poker player you must remember that the random distribution of the cards dictates that losing is inevitable for everybody. The best starting hand in Texas Hold'em is a pair of aces. But in a game where nine other people have called to see the flop, computer simulations have shown that pocket aces will only win the hand about 33 percent of the time. Even though you have the best chance of winning the pot, odds are that somebody in that group is going to beat you. In a field of nine callers, you are only going to win with the best possible starting hand one out of three times. The trick is not to let that affect you, or your game.

An important question to ask yourself while getting kicked around is, Why is this happening to me? This isn't a query to the gods in the hopes of acquiring some insight into the notion of divine justice. You're just trying to figure out why you're losing all of your money. Are you playing badly, are you being outplayed, or have you just hit a streak of bad luck? Only after you answer that question will you be able to figure out what to do next.

A lot of guys I know run straight to the cashier to buy more chips after they go bust. Even though you have to admire their fortitude, this is usually a historic blunder. Playing from behind is a very difficult thing to do. The idea that they are "down" for the evening frustrates people. They place heavy emphasis on the outcome of that one night, and their desperation to get even is palpable. Which is, of course, a very counterproductive thing.

Poker is a macro, not a micro game. Your daily performance is inconsequential. You should look at your profitability over the long haul—a year, or ten, or a lifetime. Adopting that attitude takes the emphasis off just one hand or one session and makes playing from behind much easier.

That way you can decide whether to rebuy with a clear head. The time to buy more chips is if you are clearly the best player at the table and you are just having a run of bad luck. You actually have a shot at recovering your money. If you are outmatched at the table (and almost everybody is at some point), then just go home and come back another day.

Watching somebody walk away from a table without any chips always fills me with mixed emotions. Part of me is happy; if they've lost, I've probably won. But there's another part of me that truly sympathizes. You lose your last hand, and you just sit there for a second. The other players are kind of uncomfortable, so nobody looks at you. The next hand is being dealt, and when asked if you want to keep playing, you have to say, "I've had enough fun for one day," or something similarly stupid.

Then you try to act nonchalant while standing up. Then you think that everybody knows how terrible you're feeling and how hard you're trying not to show it. You think to yourself, Well, everybody's done this at some point, but that never helps. No two people walk away in the same manner. Some people are chipper and cheerful and thank everybody for a wonderful evening as they walk out. Even though this makes it seem like the loss was no big deal, you'll frequently find those individuals later that night in the bar around the corner doing shots of tequila, all alone.

Other players get depressed. Their heads hang lower and lower over their dwindling stack of chips as the night goes on. Perhaps this is a rational reaction: they are losing, after all. The problem is that poker is supposed to be fun. Some players get mad. I've seen people throw cards at dealers, curse out waitresses, get in fights, and worse. I even saw an ex–New York Jets linebacker tear the better part of a deck in half after a particularly bad beat. Even though all of these things make you look like a complete idiot, there are still stupider things that you can do. The worst reaction a player can have to a bad night at the poker table is to go on tilt.

After losing a big hand, a player bets and raises with garbage because he is steamed over the last game. Then he loses more, and a cycle begins. Once you tilt, there's almost no hope for recovery.

Tilting is analogous to a tennis player losing a game because of a few bad breaks and then suddenly deciding that the rest of the match will be played with the racket in his opposite hand with every swing taken at his maximum strength. There's not much chance of winning that game.

I pride myself on never tilting, but the funny thing is, I tilt all the time. I just rationalize it better than most. I used to play in a $2,000 buy-in limit Hold'em game with all these fancy Wall Street guys. When I first heard about the game, I thought it would be easy pickings. As it turned out, most of the guys there had played professional poker at one time or another. Between John Tear, Damon Rein, and Brad and Andrew Moss, it was probably the toughest game I'd ever played in. I've won more money than I've lost there, but it's a lot of work. If I didn't like those guys so much, I'd be an idiot for playing with them.

There was one night when I got myself into a large hand with Brad Moss. I was already down about fifteen hundred at that point and was on the verge of beginning to play poorly, when it looked like my night was about to turn around. I was dealing, and Brad was under the gun. He raised. Only one player, a futures trader named Roy, had called before it was my turn to act.

I looked at my pocket cards. I dealt myself $J_\heartsuit J_\spadesuit$. I chose to make another raise. Brad and Roy matched my bet. The flop came $J_\clubsuit 4_\spadesuit 5_\clubsuit$. It's hard not to smile when I flop top set, but I managed to control myself and stared directly at the cards, trying desperately not to give anything away. Brad checked, Roy bet, and I raised. But instead of just calling, or folding, Brad actually followed his check by raising me. After Roy folded his cards, I raised again, making the fourth and final bet. In my defense, I didn't even try to put Brad on a hand at that point because I had the nuts. I didn't think his cards could make a difference. The turn card was the $3_\clubsuit$. Brad checked, so I bet and he raised me again. This time I took a second to think about his hand. He raised before the flop. Then the cards came out, and he liked what he saw. Normally, given those actions, I would have put him on ace-jack, but since I had most of the jacks, I gave him an over pair (kings or queens). I chose to call instead of raise, because I didn't want him to fold before the river. That way I could raise him and get an extra bet out of the hand. The river card was another five. Thank you, God. It gave me the highest possible full house on the table. Brad check-raised me again. When he did that, I put him on the nut flush. So I raised him back, thinking that would end the game. But he didn't stop raising. When there are only two players left in a Hold'em game, there is no limit to the number of raises the players can make, so I kept raising. After we each raised four times, I finally figured out that he had quad fives. I looked down and saw that I had about $100 left from my two-grand buy-in. That's when I asked him if I could just go all in and bet what I had left in front of me. Having the nuts, Brad kindly agreed.

I bet the hundred; he called and turned over his four fives. I already knew what he had, but I couldn't just sit there with twenty lonely chips in front of me after he hit his only out in the deck to beat me. I threw away $100 so I could walk out of the room and not have to watch him stack my chips. For a long time I thought I did the right thing that night, the manly thing. I even told people the story so I could cap it off with how cool I was. But the bottom line is that I knew I was beat, yet I still gave a very rich man $100 of my relatively hard-earned dollars for absolutely no reason. A great player would have folded his hand and not even called the last raise. But I didn't have to be a great player. I just had to be a non-idiot. I should have called his final raise, cashed in my chips, and gone home with another $100 in my pocket. There's no other way to see it—I tilted.

Losing does weird things to card players. I've watched a lot of people adopt personality traits radically different to those they display in their normal lives. I know a gregarious but shy Brazilian grandmother who becomes a braggart when she's down money. There's an effeminate theater critic who turns into a brute

after a bad beat and a gentle first-grade teacher who shorts the
pot whenever he starts to lose.

Chip Adler (a.k.a. Holy Chip) is a another perfect example.
During the day, he is a kind and decent Episcopal minister from
Maine who devotes most of his time to helping other people. But
at night, Holy Chip becomes something completely different. Sit
him down at a green felt table, and the man turns into some kind
of biblical serpent. He marks cards, shorts the pot, skims chips,
peeks at the cards. It's one of the strangest things I have ever seen.
He's a lovely person, but he's a terrible card cheat. The funny
thing is that he looks deeply guilty when the game is over. I often
suspect that he runs straight to the confessional after leaving the
table. But nothing is as remarkable as what happens to the shrink,
Dr. Liam Kelly, when he begins to part with his money.

"I tilt. I know I tilt," he says.

The irony is that I run a group therapy session for veterans devoted to anger management, and still sometimes mine gets the
best of me. I know, it doesn't make any sense. There is a school of
thought in psychology that preaches prophylactic intervention.
You recognize the potential for a detrimental tendency—fear, rage,
dishonesty—and you confront it by repeatedly re-creating the situation instead of avoiding it. Holy Chip is a perfect example.

A lot of shrinks would simply tell him to avoid gambling of
any sort. That's a simple solution, but I assume that his problem
is symptomatic of something deeper. If it had to do with anything but gambling, I would say that he should confront the issue

in therapy or analysis sessions. But even though I am a huge proponent of the therapeutic process, I would lean toward abstention rather than retribution. He should flat-out abstain from any competition involving money. He gets really depressed when he doesn't win the lottery. It's very deep-seated. I'm not sure the impact poker or gambling has on the personality can ever be altered. I say that because I was—as part of my Ph.D.—subjected to years of therapy and analysis, and my problem has, if anything, gotten worse.

He is of course referring to his tendency to tilt.

The term tilt comes from pinball machines. If you shake them too much in an effort to alter the path of the ball, the machine will tilt. It shuts down, and you lose your ball. The newer machines don't tilt right away; they offer a warning, let you know that you're close. That's what Dr. Liam does. At the beginning of every poker session, he is always in a fantastic mood. He's all smiles, talking about sports or the weather. But after his first loss in which he was the favorite going into the hand, he begins to shut down. His headphones go on. Conversation ends. The table has been warned. One more bad beat, and he's done.

I play a lot of poker, six nights a week when my schedule is normal. I play enough hands that statistics should hold true for me, and yet, somehow, they never do. It's beyond logic. I play about five hundred hands of poker per week. And only about twice during that time do I ever play by a hunch. Since I play so often, and almost always play according to the odds, statistically, I should end up a winner. That's because I'm competing against individuals who don't conform to statistically correct play. That's why I get so angry. Because I'm not supposed to lose.

People who have been playing with me for years don't realize that I feel it coming on when I'm about to tilt. I try to fend it off by reading. That's why I always have a book with me at the games. But it usually doesn't help. It's not how bad the beat I take is, or how many I take, it usually has to do with how quickly they follow one another. If I take two or three right in a row, I should just go home right away. And sometimes I do. But most of the time I don't. I stay and play like a jackass.

When he tilts, he loses the ability to think rationally. His temporary dementia goes way beyond a simple mood swing. Dr. Liam actually comes across as disoriented, despairing, and dangerous.

"I keep a poker journal. Do you know that when you have pocket aces, if you're playing against just one other person, you're supposed to win 88 percent of the time? In 1998, my winning percentage in that scenario was about 75 percent. Way below the expected outcome. And it has nothing to do with how I played the cards. Eighty-eight percent is purely statistical. My cards simply don't hold up as often as they are statistically supposed to. How do you explain that?"

Having that fact in his arsenal of poker knowledge isn't much of a help to Liam. It almost validates his anger. Once he begins to lose, he flushes his very intelligent and very successful game plan of playing by the numbers right down the toilet and starts to conduct himself like an amateur.

> I get mad because I play so conservatively, so by the book, in a world of even distribution, I should win. I just should. I should win because other people play worse than I do. They approach the game without logic. Sometimes without an iota of common sense. They make ill-advised calls, irrational raises, and I take advantage of that—that is, when the distribution of the cards allows me to. If I raise with an ace-jack, and some idiot calls behind me with a king-jack, he's basically drawing to three outs in the entire deck. His three miserable kings. That's it. I'm something like a three-to-one favorite. And if a jack comes on the flop, forget about it. He's gonna get killed. But, of course the flop comes king-rag-rag, and I get crushed. Listen, I don't lose money at poker. Over the past seven years I'm probably the second or third biggest winner at the club. The problem is I should win more. And that gets me mad.

Another practical application of Liam's irrational tilted state is his tendency to lecture. After a bad beat, he is famous for elaborate diatribes aimed at the person who just played badly and beat him. He spouts statistics and theories to show how improperly the person played and how lucky he was for taking Liam's hard-earned money. This is wildly counterintuitive. If Liam does really believe in the theory of probability, then he should want the person to continue playing against the odds, because eventually he'll give back everything he's won.

I know that criticizing players is counterproductive. I do it, and this may sound incredibly stupid, but it feels remarkably good to tear into somebody after they display stupidity and get rewarded for it. Listen, it's not so much *what* I do, it's *why* I do it. I feel almost conspired against. I did everything right, and some divine power rewarded somebody who didn't. And I'm not a paranoid. I have no persecution fantasies in my life.

It's very common for people with gambling problems to lose intentionally. They play badly to punish themselves, as if they don't deserve to win. You hear that over and over again in GA meetings. Addicts experience the sensation of being unloved. They gamble to qualify that in a way. If they lose, as most do, then they affirm their sense of worthlessness. They feel they deserve to lose, and it's their punishment. But I'm not like that, nor are most of the volatile card players I know. It's more like the phenomenon of transsexuals. Some female transsexuals who were molested by members of the opposite sex feel compelled to join that sex as protection. Maybe I tilt and play badly to be more like my tormenters. Who really knows, there's got to be some reason.

Maybe.

CHEATING

*He would cut the cards if he was
playing poker with his mother.*

—CHARLIE CHAPLIN

I don't know why most people decide to become card cheats. I assume it's for the money. Perhaps some of them do it just to see if they can, who knows? I can only tell you why I became one. I was a hard-up fourteen-year-old losing in an epic game of strip poker. If ever necessity was the mother of invention, that was it. Down to my tighty-whiteys and a lonely sock, I had what some might call an epiphany while shuffling the cards before my deal. I couldn't help but notice that everybody was much more interested in the goings-on at the table than what I was doing with the cards. There was my first lesson in gambling dishonesty: distraction is the key to sleight of hand.

At the time I didn't know anything about palming cards, stacking decks, fake fan shuffles, or any of the other techniques I've become familiar with over time. I just cheated by employing a little common sense. There were six people at the table (three guys, three girls), and since it was my deal, I realized that I would be getting the sixth card from the top of the deck. So I shuffled and kept looking at as many cards as possible until I located a 2. Then I cut the deck so that the 2 was on top and placed five more cards on top of it. After that, I called a game of five-card draw, 2s wild, and began to deal. I was sitting behind a pile of clothes in no time.

From what I've gathered from talking to cardsharps and deck mechanics, there is no formal training regimen to become a cheat. There are some books and an occasional seminar (more on how to spot cheating, but they do help teach techniques as well), but as far as I know, no one ever went to a school to hone his skills at stacking a deal. Sleight of hand is learned in one way—by practicing and repetition. Every unoccupied moment of the day—waiting for the bus, watching television—has got to be seen as an opportunity to improve your skills.

Perhaps the greatest card manipulator ever to live is a man named Darwin Ortiz. Darwin has said that since his early teens he has practiced card manipulation for roughly forty hours a week. Cuts, dealing, card spotting, shuffling . . . Darwin actually dropped out of law school to have more time to work on his manual dexterity. There is practically nothing he can't do with a deck.

Mr. Ortiz's most notable characteristic is that he's not a card cheat. He earns his keep by teaching casinos and law enforcement agencies how to spot gambling irregularities. But it's rare to find somebody with his skill that has a conscience. Make no mistake, cheating is rampant. If you've played cards with more than five people in your life, odds are you've been in the presence of something crooked at some point. Even if it's as simple as spotting the bottom card on the deck, everybody has cheated at one time or another.

That shouldn't be a surprising revelation because the fact of the matter is, poker was created by card cheats. Most historians see the game as this beautiful microcosm of American history, an amalgam of immigrant cultures brought to this great country by satchels and haversacks on board steamships and sailing vessels during the early 1800s. I guess that's partly true, but the inventors were a far cry from the hardworking European ancestors upon whose broken backs this country was built. Poker was conjured out of the smoke-filled air of the saloons of the South by drunks, thieves, and gunfighters.

The cards as we know them were probably brought to America sometime around 1795 by the Spanish conquistadors. The first ancestor of modern poker—and this is very open to argument—is said to have appeared in New Orleans around the late 1820s when Persian traders introduced pioneers to the card game Âs. The story goes that when engaged in a game, the settlers, who were French, would announce a wager by saying the word *poque* in place of "bet." Some card historians posit that Âs adopted some of the rules of a Central European (probably German) bluffing game known as poken. The two terms morphed together to form *pokas*.

Those facts are completely open to speculation, as I have read slight variations of them in differing orders in at least ten other poker books. The only thing that can be agreed upon is that the game then spread up along rivers, railroads, and wagon trails to every part of the country. Add a Yankee inflection and a couple of sips of whiskey to *pokas,* and the game played in taverns from Baltimore to Bangor became known as poker.

By 1840 a complete fifty-two-card deck had replaced the original twenty- and thirty-two-card versions that had been brought here by traders. A few years after that, the five-card flush was introduced. The biggest changes came during the Civil War. Thousands of American men waiting around in each other's company for months on end provided a perfect situation for countless other poker variations to be invented. Games began to be played with open cards (as in stud poker), straights (which beat a flush at that time), and draws. The joker appeared sometime around 1875. Every twist and modification of the game that came later—such as the straight flush, jackpots, qualifying hands, and extra draws—was a purely home-grown innovation.

One historical account estimated that of the 50,000 poker players who stalked New Orleans and the Mississippi riverboats during poker's early years, perhaps at most seven were honest players. The enforcement of fair play was often up to the captain or the players themselves.

There are countless stories of riverboat operators throwing crooked players into the Mississippi, and brave passengers like Alamo hero James Bowie who came to the aid of a young passenger cheated out of $50,000 by pulling his now-famous Bowie knife after spotting crooked play. But for every one of those tales, historians believe, ten captains and passersby were on the take.

Back then cheating was very unsubtle. Marked decks, one of the favorite tools of cardsharps, were so common and accepted that in the mid-1800s nationally known playing card manufacturers would advertise their marked decks on the same posters and billboards they used to promote their fair cards. Their popularity was for the most part due to the fact that marked decks were the form of cheating that required the least skill. Almost anybody could use them; the only tough part was getting the deck into the game.

Jimmy Altman, a small-time gambler from Nevada, is said to be the only person to ever get a dirty deck into Bugsy Siegel's famous game at the Flamingo. Altman had the assistance of three accomplices to run his scam. It began with a unknown gentleman walking into the Flamingo gift shop and buying every pack of cards in the store. About an hour later, Mr. Altman himself entered the store and asked to buy a pack of cards. He, of course, was told by the cashier that they were sold out.

Altman then went upstairs and sat down at the game. Right around the time the first hand was being dealt, Altman's second accomplice entered the gift shop and also requested a deck. When he was told by the shopkeeper that all the cards were sold out, the accomplice became very angry and berated the man. The store owner, incredibly apologetic, swore he would remedy the situation as soon as possible.

About an hour into the big game, Altman started to examine the cards that they were playing with. He didn't make an accusation about their fairness, he just made sure that the other players could see that he was checking them out. At the exact same time, the third partner walked into the hotel shop, handed the man behind the desk a business card, and introduced himself as a playing card salesman. The proprietor was so relieved that he bought every deck the salesman had to offer. Each one, of course, was obviously marked.

After noticing Altman looking at the cards so intensely, other players at Siegel's game began to do the same thing. Finally Altman asked to play with a new deck. When a fresh deck was opened, Altman politely asked if someone could just run down to the hotel gift shop and buy a few decks from there. All the other players agreed, and Altman took the game for almost one million dollars.

Another way to introduce a marked deck into a game is to mark the cards during play. Some mechanics have hands like tool sets. One fingernail is often so sharp it could cut skin. It's used to put creases or dots on important cards. A card cheat will often rub down his thumb and index finger with sandpaper to enhance sensitivity. That way a mechanic can read the marks like Braille while he deals them out.

People say that the mark of a good scam is that the con artist is miles away when the pigeon realizes that he got taken. The mark of a great scam is that the con artist can stay right where he is, because the pigeon never figures out what went down. That's the problem with marked cards. You have to get them out of the game after you've made your money. After he's won a few big hands a good mechanic will often point out the imperfections on the cards himself, usually after some other player has won a huge pot. That way he gets to look like the solid citizen, while the suspicion falls on the player who just won.

A good grifter will also always have an arsenal of pat lines and sound bites prepared for any situation. I once found a few hand-marked cards in my home game in grad school. Of the seven people at the table, six of us had been playing together for the better part of a year. Therefore, all the suspicion fell on the one newcomer. Before I even had the chance to accuse him, he said, "I know it's easy to blame the new guy, but is this the first time you've noticed creases in the cards?" The answer to that is always no. Cards get creased all the time. So his little redirection of suspicion worked perfectly as a group of six friends began to think about all the other times we had to change decks in the middle of the game because a card suddenly had a crease or a dimple. He was so convincing that we actually let the guy keep playing with us for a couple of weeks before he disappeared.

I don't know what we would have done if we'd actually caught him doing something underhanded. It probably would have resulted in a bunch of prep-school shoving and macho posturing before somebody stepped in and broke it up. That's because my friends and I are civilized, not to mention wusses, which is probably why that guy chose our game. But getting caught in clubs and casinos can often result in a lot worse treatment. I've seen a player have $6,000 confiscated because he pinched a hundred-dollar chip from the pot. I've also heard stories about players getting roughed up on suspicion alone.

The repercussions of cheating were much worse back in the Wild West. A legendary American Indian poker player named Poker Tom was said to have cheated a California merchant named Ah Tia out of $2,000. Two days later, the remains of Poker Tom were apparently fed to members of his own tribe in a stew that Ah Tai had cooked himself at a county fair.

That's why loaded dice and marked decks are the most idiotic scams of all time. Getting caught with such hard evidence leaves very little wiggle room. There's no way to argue when somebody cracks open your die and pulls out a weight. Identifying a marked deck is as simple as riffling through the cards as if you're looking at an old-fashioned moving picture book. The subtle differences on the back of the cards will always flash as the cards flip by.

Sleight of hand leaves almost no evidence. It's pretty tough for someone else to prove that you've been bottom dealing, or stacking the deck. Somebody might turn over your card and show that you dealt yourself an ace, but that's hardly DNA evidence. Lots of people get dealt aces, and almost all of them didn't get them by cheating. A sturdy denial will usually get you out of harm's way, unless, of course, you are an idiot like me.

When I was at graduate school in Connecticut, I bartended at a place called the Cardinal Pub two nights a week. On Sundays my boss would close the bar early and invite a few friends over for a poker game. At first I was asked to serve the players. But on a night when the game was short a few players, I was asked to play.

I made sure to be on my best behavior my first few times playing. But it didn't take long for me to start cheating. Since there was no shoe (the black plastic card that goes on the bottom of the deck), it was easy for me to bottom-deal. A cheater cannot cheat all the time. He has to pick and choose his spots. I limited myself to three hands a night. That edge was plenty for me to walk away a consistent winner.

I had been playing in the game for about two months before I got myself into trouble. It was late in the evening, and most of us were quite drunk. I was dealing, and I set the deck by spotting an ace during a shuffle and moving it to the bottom of the deck. I "slip-cut" (cut the cards but left the bottom card where it was) and then dealt. Halfway through distributing the cards, I noticed that my boss was staring at me. He watched the entire thing. In my pathetic drunken stupor, I forgot to be even the slightest bit smooth about manipulating the cards. He just sat there with a look of total disbelief on his face. I folded immediately, but before I could mix my discards into the deck, my boss picked up my hand and examined it. He nodded as if his suspicions were confirmed but said nothing until we were locking up the bar.

"You're not welcome to play with us anymore," he said in passing.

At first I thought about asking why and then denying the accusations. But he was a decent, hardworking man, so I decided not to insult him further. All I said was, I understand. He told me that I had two weeks to find another job. I offered to tend bar for a week at no cost to him before I left, but he refused.

"Clearly you need the money."

The worst part was that I didn't really need the money. I was at school on a tuition waver, I had a job at the observatory and the bar, and had very recently come into a decent-size inheritance. I was only cheating because I could. That was the last time I set a deck for anything other than a joke.

♠

Cheating ability isn't simply a collection of physical skills. There's more to it than manual dexterity. Mental attributes like concentration and determination are equally as important. Clearly, those were not my strong suit. It takes a fairly skill-less mechanic to get caught the way I did. But there are still card cheats with less skill than me. They do things like call a hand that they don't have. They'll say they have a flush, lay down four spades, hiding their fifth card (a club) behind the rest, and try to sweep in the pot before anybody notices. And if they're caught, they'll just apologize and say they misread their hand.

Another common method of low-level cheating is to short the pot. A player will throw $8 worth of chips into the pot when the bet is $10. Once the chips are in with the rest, how can you tell how much he wagered?

Unaesthetic cheating methods like these are looked down upon by highly skilled mechanics. A great cardsharp will call shorting the pot "cheating," while he considers a maneuver that requires a great amount of skill like setting a deck as "just part of the game." A talented cheat thinks that since his method is refined, it's less egregious or dirty. This never made much sense to me. Stealing is stealing. I have a friend named Eric who always justifies his dalliances with prostitutes by saying how gorgeous the woman was. What's the difference? He's still sleeping with a hooker.

One huge advantage great cardsharps have over hacks like me

is that they have to cheat a lot less often. They're so good at what they do that when they choose to stack the cards, they can create much more profitable scenarios. I could only cheat during my deal, and I could only place one card at a time. So once per round I could provide myself with a wild card or an ace. This is obviously an advantage, but in no way does it guarantee a profit. For my marginal skills to translate into money worth the time and the potential damage to my reputation, I would have to try to set the deck every time I had the cards in my hands.

A skilled manipulator, someone who can place a series of cards, needs to do it only two or three times a night. Those few hands are almost guaranteed winners, and that should give him plenty of edge. Most card cheats, aside from having phenomenal tactile dexterity, are good cardplayers. They're probably a little unorthodox, perhaps overly aggressive, but then again, they can afford to be. They assume that they are going to get better cards than the rest of the table. And in the worst circumstance, if they are taking a huge bath, they can just set the deck again and make up their losses on their next deal.

Master cardsharps will only set a deck once during a night. That's all they need. With their excessive skill, they can not only give themselves a great hand but set up patsy hands as well. They'll spread out great hands across the table. Give two other players full houses and deal themselves quads. That way they are assured not only of the win, but a huge win at that.

There are basically four parts to manipulating the deck. The first and most obvious is choosing the right time to cheat. You have to have access to the cards. Once you get hold of them, the second challenge is to find the cards in the deck you care to use. That is relatively easy when you're playing a game with exposed cards like stud or Hold'em, where there are a lot of cards faceup on the board. After the hand, you just sweep up the discards and either leave them alone and memorize their order, or organize them in the order you want.

The act of going through the muck and looking for cards is called "rabbit hunting." It is the easiest time to spot a cheater. But remember, if the mechanic is skilled, you'll never see him organizing the cards. It'll just look like he scooped them up normally.

In knowing the order of the cards, a player doesn't even have to reset or manipulate the order in which they are going to be dealt to gain an advantage. If a player were to take the five up cards from a previous hand of Texas Hold'em, place them on top of the deck, fake shuffle, and then fake the cut, he would then know half the hand of the first five players in the game. That's a huge advantage. And even if his fake cut doesn't work, and another player cuts the deck, he'll realize that those five cards are buried so deep that they will never come into play in the hand. So if he buried two queens and he's got one in his hand, he knows he's not drawing very well and will fold his cards. He did not win the pot, but by cheating, he saved himself from a probable loss. And that's just as good.

The mechanic's work is not done after he simply locates the cards in the deck. That's actually the easy part. Once he knows where the cards are, then he has to stack them in the deck in such a way that he's going to deal himself or his partner a pat hand. And then finally he has to beat the cut.

The most basic form of fake shuffling is a maneuver called an overhand tumble or overhand spread. The cards are taken in one hand, pulled out of the middle of the deck in bunches, and then placed on the bottom. That way the top cards are undisturbed. So if the mechanic had placed three 5s on the top, they will still be there at the end of his shuffle. If you can picture it, you'll understand why it isn't very hard to spot. It's a very amateur way of setting a deck. You'd have to be at a very friendly or very drunken game to pull this off without being spotted.

There also is a technique called a *false* or *jab shuffle*. This is done by splitting the deck into two, then shuffling the cards back together. But instead of squaring the mixed cards and just leaving them that way, the cheat pushes the cards through one end, out the other, and then returns them to the order they were in before the mix. This is much harder to notice. If you get good at this, you're almost never going to be caught. It's hard to see even if you're doing nothing but staring at the deck.

"Riffle" or "fan" shuffling is the most common way to mix cards. It's done when the deck is split in two parts and then is mixed back together so that the cards interlace. If a cheat is good enough to be able to move cards while doing this, the other players at the table are in deep trouble. The cheat can remember where the cards started out and then move them around by counting how many cards have fallen on top of it. You're never going to see him do anything suspicious during the shuffle. If you suspect a person of setting a deck, the only thing you can do to protect yourself is leave, or make sure that there is a fair cut. Just separate the deck into two parts and have another player place the bottom half on the top. That's called a clean cut.

One easy way to beat the cut is to have a partner in crime at the table. One of the team members will set the deck, then hand the cards to his partner. The partner looks like he's cutting the deck, but he is actually moving the cards around for show. When he returns the cards to the dealer, they will be in the exact same order as they were when his partner set the deck. Team play is also a huge advantage because you're always guaranteed a lot of action if you have a good hand. There's no worse feeling in the world than having a huge hand and never seeing a bet or a raise. Partners will always raise each other, creating a big pot and luring would-be chasers in.

Another advantage to playing as a team is the ability to pass cards. I worked with a partner a bit in grad school. We had a method of signaling each other by chip stacking and placing. Let's say we were playing draw. My partner pretends that he's counting his chips and breaks down the stacks. In doing that, he's telling me what's in his hand. Let's say he tells me he's got two pairs, eights and sevens. If I have either of those cards in my hand, I signal him back by blowing two smoke rings. That way he knows his full house is coming. I palm the necessary card from my hand when it's his turn to draw, place it on top of the deck, and deal it to him. Then I draw, and quickly muck my hand before anybody notices that I have one card less than everybody else. The only way this works is if I stay in to draw. It costs me money, of course, but what do I care? My partner is going to win the pot and split it up with me later.

If the cheater has set the deck—let's say he's placed three 9s on the bottom—but he's not skilled enough to organize the cards to fall where he wants them to by riffle shuffling, he then has to bottom-deal, another popular method of cheating. While holding the cards, the dealer pulls back the bottom card to peek at it using the height of the deck itself to conceal his action. If it's a card that will help him or his partner, then he saves it until it's useful. If it's a blank, and no help to anybody, then he'll place it on the hand that looks like it's developing into something dangerous.

The more skilled mechanics can go far beyond simple bottom

dealing. Some can deal the second card from the top; this is called deuce dealing. If the mechanic has any skill at all, this is a hard method to spot. The cheat will slide the top two cards off the top of the deck slightly with the thumb of the hand holding the deck and using the forefinger of the other hand to slide the second card from the top out. It can be pretty slick; but there are a couple of tells in this method. First, the thumb is a dead giveaway. Usually, people dealing a straight game lift their thumb off the deck every time they deal a card. A deuce dealer's thumb moves side to side rather than up and down. Also, there is the sound. Dealing a fair hand usually makes no noise at all. If you're dealing the second card, it's hard not to make a scraping sound when the card comes out.

Some great cheats can even deal a card from the middle of the deck. But the mechanic can sometimes blow this scam as well. Too often the card gets partially stuck in the deck and he'll fumble it, or worse, he'll deal nothing but air. This is why it's best to play with a "shoe," or plastic bottom card, that prevents most bottom dealing or peeking.

Catching a cheat is a tough thing to do. The only evidence is usually a good hand, which of course could have been dealt to the mechanic by chance. If you accuse somebody of cheating, odds are it isn't going to be pretty. You're better off just changing tables or talking to the management or whoever is running the game and informing them of your suspicions.

I suspect that what I am about to say will make me sound like I'm an apologist for the scum who stalk card clubs and private games, taking advantage of unsuspecting strangers. But sometimes cheating isn't the cardsharp's fault—the pigeons occasionally come to you. There you are, minding your own business, playing a fair game, and somebody sits down right next to you, introduces themselves, smiles, and basically invites you take advantage of them.

It happened to me a couple of months after my boss caught me cheating at the Cardinal Pub. I was playing in a game of Hold'em in the Sahara Hotel in Vegas. The stakes were embarrassingly tiny, $2–$4, and the participants were far from well-off. Seated directly to my right was an older woman, maybe eighty, whose grandchildren were watching her play.

Every time this old woman checked her pocket cards, she held them up and out in front of her to compensate for her farsightedness. My hand to God, I wasn't trying to cheat. I wasn't even trying to make money in that game, I was just killing time. I'd gotten crushed at the dice tables and was waiting for my friends to finish up their rolls so we could go to dinner. But what was I supposed to do? She flashed me her cards every hand.

Since I'd sworn off underhandedness after losing my job, this woman presented an interesting moral dilemma. There were many factors to consider. First, this woman was a terrible player.

She was going to lose her money anyway. The second issue to take into account was that at the time, I was still considering playing poker professionally. If I was going to make a living at the game, there was no way I could let a profitable situation like this get away from me. After an elaborate internal debate, I decided not to look at her cards, but just to take her money on the up and up.

The only problem with my solution was that this woman kept showing me her cards, and well, she beat me two hands in a row. So I peeked. What can I say, I was losing. Finally I won a few pots, but then I was suddenly hit by an overwhelming wave of guilt. I began to wonder if the $40 I was going to win was worth eternity in hell. So I got up and left. But in all honesty, to this day, I genuinely think that I did the wrong thing in leaving the table. What any pro will tell you is that you cannot give up that seat. In fact, when I did leave, someone else sat down. And that person took that old lady's money instead of me. The way you have to think about it is that she's going to lose her entire buy-in no matter who's sitting next to her. You have to become desensitized to that sort of thing. You can't let it bother you.

John Powell was a riverboat poker player in the mid-1800s, perhaps one of four honest ones to play in those times. When he was fifty his net worth was estimated at $500,000, a lot of money at that time. And this man had never held an honest job in his life. He played a young English traveler in a saloon in New Orleans and proceeded to take every penny the man had plus his luggage. The Englishman was very polite, shook Powell's hand after the game, and went upstairs to his room. The next day the man returned, greeted everyone, and then, in front of Powell and the others, pulled a gun and shot himself. Powell was so disturbed that he sent the young man's widow the money and luggage and quit gambling for over a year. When he returned, he found that he was nothing like the player that he was before, and within three years he was completely broke. A conscience can be the downfall of many a good player.

An ability to cheat is not necessary to being a winner, though even a great player like Johnny Moss has admitted to cheating mercilessly in his early years. Somebody like world champion Erik Seidel, a pure gentleman, has probably never thought about behaving unscrupulously at a card table. Faced with my situation with the kindly grandmother, he probably would have told the old lady that he could see her cards, helped her correct the problem, and then check-raised her on the very next hand. Erik is a savage player. He'll never let up on you, no matter how over-matched or lost you look at a table. He's a pure predator. But that's what makes him so successful. I'm not sure I have that in me. That's probably the reason why, no matter how much I play, I'll never be one of the greats.

BIG-TIME PROS

In order to play high-stakes poker, you need to have a total disregard for money. The only time you notice it is when you run out.

—DOYLE BRUNSON,
winner of the 1976 and 1977 World Series of Poker

Like any vocation, poker has its celebrities. Average players tend to look up to their celebrated counterparts. They treat them the same way extras in a movie treat the stars. Low-limit players like me stand around holding our racks of $5 chips, watching the big guys play, oohing and ahing at every raise and re-raise they make like we're watching Fourth of July fireworks. We fantasize that one day our racks will be filled with thousand-dollar markers, and those great players we idolize will nod at us respectfully as we sit at their tables. That's the fantasy anyway. In truth, the odds of a poker player becoming one of the legends is thousands of times worse than one of the extras becoming a movie star.

I've met some of the greats, even played with a couple. Some are polite and humble, others are absurd and seem like cartoon caricatures of themselves. The first time I sat down in a World Series of Poker game, I was two seats away from Erik Seidel. He was once a regular person living in New York City making a regular living in the financial sector. A few years back he moved out to Vegas to play professional poker, and many millions of dollars later, he is still as humble and polite as anybody I have ever met.

After I beat him two hands in a row (both on improbable draws on the river, and both times having check-raised him), Erik smiled and said, "That's twice you got me."

"Gee, I can't wait to tell the boys at home," I replied sarcastically.

Most big-time players would have been irritated by some nobody like me sucking out on them on the river. But Erik just laughed and said, "That was very funny." He is, however, as far as I can tell, the exception. Strange things happen to those who are successful at what he does for a living.

For a brief period in my life I thought I wanted to go to med school. That chapter quickly came to a close after I attended my first anatomy class with a real live (dead) cadaver, and then promptly threw up for the next hour straight. My professor consoled me by saying that I'd get used to the sight, that after a while I'd be able to cut into a human corpse like I was knifing into a steak. What a fantastic thought. I filed my papers to double-major in physics and astronomy later that day.

I never figured out what I thought was a worse fate: being a doctor who couldn't bear to cut into human flesh, alive or dead, or a human being that became so desensitized to it that they lost forever the almost magical appreciation I have for the human body.

Professional gamblers experience the same phenomenon— the only difference is that they lose an understanding of the value of money rather than of the human soul. A hundred-dollar chip here, a thousand-dollar raise and million-dollar prize there, it knocks the sense out of them. But just as a doctor needs to be able to overlook the humanity of his patients to be effective, a gambler needs to be able to disregard the monetary value of money. Otherwise, he'd be completely ineffective.

This is because money is different in Vegas than it is in the rest of the world. In his book, *The Biggest Game in Town*, the great writer/poker player A. Alvarez described a photographer who wandered the floor of Binion's poker room, offering to take portraits of the players for $75. Alvarez describes the difficulty the photographer encountered in scaring up business. His problem was that the commerce of Las Vegas was not used to such a strange number as 75. Fifty-dollar chips, hundred-dollar bills, now that they understood. So the photographer raised his price to $100, an amount a player could pay easily with one bill, and found that he had a lot more interest in his services.

While I was in Vegas for the World Series of Poker, I was supposed to interview another former World Series champion named Huckleberry Seed for an article I was writing for *Details* magazine. In a room filled with oddball poker-playing idiot savants with names like Amarillo Slim Preston and Puggy Pearson, Huck is considered to be the colorful one.

At the time of my very brief interview, Huck was a thirty-one-year-old Cal Tech dropout living in Las Vegas. He started making his living gambling when he was nineteen. In 1997, at the age of twenty-seven, he won the main event of the World Series and became the third-youngest player in history to hold the title of world champion.

The thing that makes Huck stand out from the rest of the poker playing carnival is his skill at proposition wagering. A prop bet can be made on anything. I'll bet you can't eat an entire jar of mayonnaise in two minutes, $50 says you can't run three miles in under a quarter of an hour, that kind of thing. No matter how bizarre the wager sounds, there is a skill to it. The savvy comes out in the odds making. The importance of the bet is not so much whether a person thinks he can eat the entire jar as whether the bettor can assess how likely he is to do it and then request a payout that represents the probability of his success. Huck is a master odds maker. If there's a 10 percent chance that he can hit the bull's-eye on a dartboard blindfolded, he makes sure that the odds he's getting are more like 20–1. That way it doesn't matter if he hits the mark or not, he's making a good bet. The theory of probability says that in the end, he'll come out a winner. That's his skill, and it's a very profitable one to have.

Huck's wagers have included learning how to do a standing backflip for $10,000 and playing basketball against a former NBA player for $17,000. He has stood on his head for fifty-two minutes and bet that he could float at sea for twenty-four hours. He even has a wager that spans thirty-five years (for $100,000 he bet legendary poker player Doyle Brunson that he'll never weigh over 250 pounds).

When I set out to interview Huck, I thought I could mix that background information in with what he said in our conversation, and I'd come out with something interesting. Being six feet, six inches tall, he's not hard to find. I spotted Huck while I was signing up to play in the World Series and approached him in the disorganized melee that precedes most big tournaments.

"I'm writing a piece on you for *Details* magazine," I said.

At first he just looked around on his own eye level, as if the question could only have come from something as tall as he is.

Then he looked down (I'm five-eight on a warm day) and acted startled to see me standing there.

"What?" he asked.

"I'm writing an article about you."

"So?" he said.

"So, I was hoping to get an interview."

"Good luck" was his reply.

I was told that that was classic Huck. Now, I understand that I'm not Bob Woodward or Norman Mailer, but this guy isn't Jonas Salk or Mother Teresa either. He's a gambler. How about showing the slightest bit of humility or gratitude? You know what, I take that back. How about just not being rude? I'm a relatively intelligent person. I'm a decent human being. *Details* didn't call me up and demand a piece on Huck Seed, I pitched it to them. I suggested the story because, from what I'd heard, Huck was an interesting guy. And deep down, I actually thought that he might be flattered that a well-respected national publication wanted to run a story on him. I was wrong. In fact, he couldn't have been less interested. He provided me with about two minutes of "yes," "no," and "I'd rather not talk about that," and then walked away. *Details* killed the piece.

A fellow writer/novelist/poker player named Peter Alson explained my encounter with Huck this way; he told me that I had to understand that this type of celebrity has no need for the media. Rock stars need the press to sell more albums. Movie stars need us to sell more tickets. Media coverage to a gambler is simply self-promotion and ego stroking. And some of them have had enough of that. That doesn't make them bad people, just bad topics for articles.

Alson's insight comes from an article he wrote a long time ago on World Champion poker player Johnny Chan. After Chan's first World Series win in 1987, *Esquire* dispatched Alson to interview him. Alson called Chan's place in Las Vegas at around 2:00 P.M. local time. Chan was still sleeping. He tried a couple more times and finally got Chan on the phone. He identified himself as a journalist writing a piece for *Esquire.*

"A story on me?" Chan asked. "Is *Esquire* the one you see in the supermarket all the time?"

"No," Alson replied. "You're thinking of the *Enquirer.*"

Alson told Chan that *Esquire* was one of the top-selling men's magazines in America. After he explained the difference between "men's magazine" and "porn magazine," Chan reluctantly agreed to the interview. They set a time and a date to sit down and talk. Chan extended an invitation to meet him at the poker room of the Mirage Hotel, in Las Vegas.

At this point, Alson was thrilled. He had secured an interview with the very elusive Johnny Chan. And beyond that, he was able to do it in such a way that he was meeting Chan on the poker player's own turf. Chan would be comfortable, maybe even open up. Alson is a great poker player himself, so he thought that maybe he'd get to play a few hands with Chan and write the article from that point of view. He packed his Dictaphone, some paper, and pens and flew off to Vegas on *Esquire*'s dollar. Alson strutted into the Mirage's poker room and asked for Chan, just like he was told to do.

There was one problem. Chan wasn't there; he had flown to Europe earlier in the week to play in a poker tournament. Alson returned to New York later that day to break the bad news to the magazine. The editor asked Alson to try one more time to conduct the interview.

When Alson finally got Chan on the phone, he asked what had happened. The answer he got was simply, "Oh, you were serious?" So they set another time and place. This time the interview was going to be conducted at Chan's home in southern California.

The writer flew west again. He rented a car in Los Angeles, drove a few hours to Chan's house, and knocked on his door. The world-famous cardplayer answered the door in a bathrobe. He shook Alson's hand and asked if he could have a few minutes to get himself together. Alson agreed and then was told to wait in his car for Chan. After about fifteen minutes, Chan knocked on Alson's window and said something like, "Okay, I've got five minutes, what do you want to know?"

My assumption is that these guys weren't always so standoffish. It's probably a result of their incredible success. I assume that Huck was peppered with interview requests after his World Series win, so I guess that makes his attitude somewhat understandable. He and Chan are true hometown celebrities. They are well known around the city. They are ogled at and whispered about when they enter a card room. They are asked for autographs, receive fan mail, and are catered to by employees of various casinos as if they were royalty.

Celebrity, along with its benefits, is not unique to gamblers. But the isolation of their success, and the precariousness of the perch from which they view the mortal world around them, is. Movie stars work with other movie stars on projects. Sports heroes who earn $10 million a year have ties to some sort of organization, be it the team that they represent or, in the case of golf or tennis, the country they periodically represent. Gambling is different. It's every man for himself.

Gamblers also face an occupational hazard unique to their line of work: the constant possibility of going broke. If Tiger Woods plays poorly for a season, nobody can take money out of his bank account to punish him. To do what they do, poker players and gamblers alike must, on almost a daily basis, risk their own resources to maintain a steady stream of income. And even the best of them make mistakes or get unlucky and go broke.

Nick "the Greek," one of the first participants in the World Series of Poker—who at many different times in his life had a net worth of over $5 million—lived out the last few years of his life practically penniless, playing $5–$10 poker. It happens to the best of them. In fact, early in the summer of 2000 I was told by a group of poker players that Huck Seed himself had gone bust and was actually having trouble borrowing startup money. If it's true, I have no doubt he'll be back; he's too good a poker player to be away for long.

Stu Unger, perhaps the greatest cardplayer of all time, bounced back from the brink many times. That's why he was known as "The Comeback Kid." As far as professional cardplayers went, he was the genuine article. Born the son of a bookie in New York City, Unger started hustling when he was thirteen. A few years later he gained the favor of the Genovese crime family, and between his card skills and their protection, Stu became the most notorious cardplayer in New York. His professional poker career started in the late 1970s; he won the Super Bowl of Poker twice and the vaunted World Series of Poker in '80, '81, and '97.

But unlike most of the other professionals I've mentioned, Stu had a firm grasp of his own limitations. He knew all too well what the life was like. After winning $350,000 in a major tournament, a reporter asked Unger what he was planning to do with the money. "Probably lose it," he replied, and eventually he did.

Though he seemed to have a realistic understanding of himself, Stu's grasp of the world around him was far from insightful. Stu did not open his first checking account until he was well into his thirties—and even after he did, he thought that he had to go to the bank every time he wanted to write a check. When he was thirty-three years old, he applied for his first passport, which he needed to travel to Ireland to play in a poker tournament. He told the clerk that he needed the passport right away. The clerk responded, "That will cost extra." Unger said, "No problem," and slipped the clerk $200 under the table. Unger almost got arrested for trying to bribe a public official. The clerk was referring to the $20 expedience fee.

The IRS estimated Unger's professional earnings at over $4 million during his career, which does not include what he made in back alleys and underground card houses. Despite this fact, he spent most of his life flat broke. The irony was that he was probably the greatest cardplayer ever, but that skill could not compensate for the fact that he was an awful, degenerate gambler. He lost hundreds of thousands of dollars playing golf with men who were much better than he was. But he played regardless because he couldn't stand the idea that there was gambling going on that he wasn't involved in.

Stu's second curse was drugs. Like a great number of professional cardplayers—in an occupation where stamina is as much

of an asset as mathematical ability or psychological insight—
Unger had a well-documented addiction to cocaine and other
amphetamines. On the morning of November 22, 1998—less
then six months after he won the World Series—when Stu was
found in a cheap motel room in downtown Vegas, dead at the age
of forty-five, many friends speculated that his death was due to
abuse of those substances. However, it should be mentioned that
no drugs or paraphernalia were found in his room. Stu had $800
in his pocket when he was found. That was all the money he had
in the world.

Drugs, overconfidence, ego, disenfranchisement, these are the
plagues of the wildly successful cardplayers. Now try to imagine
what it's like to be a lower-echelon pro.

SMALL-TIME PROS

Marriages may come and go,
but the game must go on.

—FELIX UNGER,
The Odd Couple

The oldest player at the Winchester club is a guy called Iron Mike. He's ninety-one. Whenever he's asked how he is, or what's going on, he always says, "I'm alive, ain't I? So I guess I'm a better poker player than I was yesterday, and that can't be a bad thing." The one time I asked him to elaborate on that thought, he told me, "You know, this damn game ain't baseball, or basketball, or even golf. Poker's a thing you do your whole life. I started playing when I learned to count. I always figured I'd quit when I forgot how to. And since that ain't happening yet, the older I get, the better I get. What else can you say that about? The only trick for a kid your age is to try not to waste your entire time on the planet playing this stupid game."

I read that quote to Dicky Horvath, an accountant turned professional poker player I was interviewing, and he nodded sympathetically.

"Iron Mike's right. That's the hard part," Dicky said, "not wasting your life playing the game." Dicky was born in Jersey City, New Jersey, in 1960. For all his life he has been somebody who "chose the road less traveled. I was the guy in high school who thought college was for losers. I called all those honor-roll kids headed for prestigious schools conformists and capitalist cogs. Of course it took one year of delivering pizza and working construction for me to end up at Jersey City State. Then I did the same thing with Columbia Business. After graduating college, all it took was four months of telemarketing to get me studying for my GMATs."

Dicky says his IQ has been measured at 180, though he admits that he never received an A in any school course in his life. "I got B's and C's even in the classes that I did the work for. Maybe that was because I copped an attitude with those professors, like I was angry at them for making me put in the effort. That's what's such a turn-on about poker. There's no boss, no dress-codes or time limits. There's always a game somewhere. So you're never late for anything. And the best part is that there's no grandmother in Des Moines whose life's savings you've thrown away if the market goes down. If you get slapped around at the table, you're the only one who goes hungry."

Many professional poker players are self-proclaimed prodigies. They pick up the game when they are four or five years old and never look back. That's the way Stu Unger, Johnny Moss, and Doyle Brunson came to greatness. But not Dicky Horvath. He didn't play his first hand of poker until he was twenty-four.

> I was in my first year of business school and the other degenerate in my class, a guy who called himself Grim, took me to a card club in Chinatown. I already knew the game a bit, but Grim showed me the nuances of poker that you needed to win consistently. They are easy to pick up. I swear, I could teach any idiot how to make thirty grand a year by playing poker. It's actually not that hard. All you need is patience and the ability to count to thirteen. If you can numb yourself, you're way ahead of the game. See, if you're a pro, somebody who's there to make money day in and day out, then you never take chances. Guys who come to a game to gamble or have a good time, blow off some steam, they're huge dogs to me in the long run because they are gonna take chances that don't make statistical sense. They draw to a gut shot when there's no money in the pot because they got some absurd feeling or something like that. He may get there and scoop the pot, but in the long run, that isn't anything but bad card play. That's where I make my money.

Horvath graduated toward the bottom of his class at Columbia and went on to an extremely unsatisfying two years on Wall Street in a small investment firm in New York City. "That's when I started playing a lot of poker. I played in three regular home games a week and then at the card clubs the rest of the nights. I would go straight from work to a game, play till about midnight, go home, pass out, and then start the whole thing over again. When I look back, it wasn't such a bad life. My house was a rat-hole, so I didn't mind only being there to sleep. I had no social life to speak of, I don't think I had been laid since my high school prom, so, you know, all things considered, not a bad life at all."

Being a small-time pro like Horvath does not require the same attributes that are prerequisites to becoming one of the greats. The subtlety of the game isn't as important as more working-class characteristics like patience and stamina.

There's nothing suave to being a hustler. If you watch tape of the old World Series, you'll see magician shit. Doyle reading Johnny Chan's body language and folding a huge hand. Or Johnny suckering Erik Seidel—probably the best player in the world—into calling when Johnny had the nuts. But that's not what I do. My gig is to be like a drone. Some mindless ant worker. I have to play mechanically, not seductively. That's because I'm not there for a game. How I do on any one day doesn't mean shit. I'm playing in a year-long poker game. I can never get emotional. If you look at my poker log, you'll see that I have good days and bad days, good months and not so good months. But in the end, as the number of hands increase, the variations are actually pretty small.

Excerpt from Dicky Horvath's Diary

Date	Stakes	Place	Time	Outcome	Year to Date
1/6/96	10–20	Winch.	3 hours	+170	+170
1/7/96	3 max	Tom's	2.5 hours	+55	+225
1/9/96	4–8	Heart	2 hours	-50	+175
1/9/96	15–30	Win.	5 hours	+378	+553
1/10/96	10–20	Heart	3 hours	-200	+353
1/11/96	10–20$\frac{1}{2}$ kill	The Taj	4 hours	+150	+503
1/12/96	10–20$\frac{1}{2}$ kill	The Taj	3.5 hours	+102	+605
1/12/96	20–40	The Taj	3 hours	+1,156	+1,771
1/13/96	10–20$\frac{1}{2}$ kill	The Taj	5 hours	-250	+1,521
1/16/96	10–20	Winch.	3 hours	+65	+1,686
1/17/96	5 max	Peter's	2 hours	-25	+1,661

In 1995 Dicky quit his job and began to play poker full-time. "But make no mistake, being a professional poker player is a job like any other. That's when you get in deep shit, when you start to look at it as work. After a while you look at your poker log and you start to see a per-hour wage. It gets you thinking about how much time you waste doing other things. You start to think about life as a poker game. That movie cost me fifty bucks because I could have been playing instead. That's when you're fucked."

That summer, Dicky moved down to Atlantic City to have access to games around the clock. "I could play twenty, thirty, forty hours at a time. Remember, the more you play, the more you make. My greatest asset in poker is that I've always been pretty unemotional. So I'll have my pocket aces snapped and not think twice about it, while the guy across the table from me will go crazy. Raise, raise, raise. He tilts, you know, plays like an asshole, and I stay cool and take his chips. I love those guys."

But that kind of lifestyle has an impact on any individual. "The monotony is what kills you. Not the gambling. You got to remember that poker is a finite game. There are only so many variations. I've been dealt pocket aces five hands in a row. That's like a billion to one odds. I figured it out once. In a game of seven-card stud, I saw two guys chop a pot because they both had 10-high straight flushes. You play enough, and you're going to see everything. It's actually pretty boring, that's why there are no good poker movies. The game is a bore to watch. Two things started to happen to me when I moved to AC. I became numb to the game, which is sort of a good thing, but then I tried to become un-numb, and that was a bad thing."

Seeking out distractions from the grind of poker, Horvath began to take drugs.

> I partied with Stu Unger a long time ago in Vegas. . . . Maybe partied is the wrong word. We never did drugs for fun, they were always there to keep us up or bring us down. But never just for fun. I started with coke and amphetamines because they kept you juiced at the table. You know that old anti-coke commercial about the circular logic of doing blow? That was me: I do blow

so I can play more poker, so I can make more money, so I can buy more blow, so I can play more poker. And it worked for a while.

But that was just the beginning. The only thing I looked forward to about playing cards was what drug I was going to do at the table. Trust me, there's nothing else to do. I tried reading, counting, memorizing, I even cut a hole in the pocket of my jeans so I could jerk off at the table. I swear, I could jerk off right next to a rabbi, and he'd never know. But even that got boring after a while. Playing poker for a living is a total grind. There's no fun or variation in your play. You can never act on a hunch. Everything is by the book. You're like a robot. Being smart or creative is actually a drawback.

That's why guys like me who grind out winnings stick to limit games. There's a huge difference. In limit there is very little flair or psychology. You play your cards by statistics and never do things on a hunch. No-limit is all touch and guts. In limit if three people call your raise and you've got pocket aces, and the flop comes king, 10, 4, you bet out and some guy raises and then he keeps betting, you just call him down to the river to see if he's got a set or maybe two pair, kings and 10s. But in no-limit, you bet out with your aces and he raises your entire stack. What are you going to do then? That's when business school looks really appealing. In limit Hold'em a mistake like calling that guy down is only going to cost you three bets, maybe $60, $100 in the worst scenario, but in no-limit, a fuckup like that could burn you for your entire buy-in. You'll be in the poker hospital for months after that bad call. Nope, to make a living like I do, you have to stick to good old boring limit Hold'em. It is the only way to go. And trust me, drugs are the only solution to that situation. You just have to figure out what kind of mood you're in. Coke, valium, acid, heroin, it's going to make a difference in how you play. Though you'd have to stay out of Circus-Circus Casino if you were tripping.

No matter how awful his life sounds, Horvath claims that it was, in his mind, a success. "You know, when I tell it like this, I guess it sounds kind of gruesome, but you know what? When I was in the middle of it, it felt great. I was making money, having shit-loads of fun. I even fell in love."

The woman he met was a poker dealer from Atlantic City named Dolly. "Dolly was this beautiful brunette, stone-cold bitch of a woman. She was absolutely the nuts. I never met anybody like her in my life. She was all about plans. Put this much money away, we'll be able to move to some place and buy some kind of house. But if we put more money away, then we can move to some nicer place and get some nicer house. As soon as I'd walk into the apartment, she'd make me empty my pockets. In '96 I placed well in a couple of big Hold'em tournaments, and she was right there to pick up the check. My big mistake was teaching her how to play poker well."

Dolly's thought pattern was simple to follow. Horvath was making about $35 an hour by playing poker and paying no taxes on the money. She was making $20 (plus tips) as a dealer, but the government was taking a large percentage of her income. "Once I taught her how to play to win, she quit her job. She figured with both of us playing, we could double our income. And for a while, she was right. We moved out to Vegas, and for three months we were living huge out there. We were putting two grand in cash away every week. It was a dream. But then she got caught up in the same shit that I did. The boredom, the monotony. I swear, there isn't a Hindu monk alive that could deal with how boring limit poker gets. So she started the drugs like me. I think it was the summer of '96 that we both became coke addicts. Though you never know you're an addict while you're using. It's only when you stop using that you figure it out. And then, you know, the wheels are off. All the money disappears. You start playing bad. And then you're in a hole. You start borrowing, and then the hole gets deeper and deeper."

Dolly was the first to enroll in a rehabilitation program. She checked into an inpatient program in Los Angeles and returned to Las Vegas in August of 1997 clean and sober. "When she came back I was totally shocked. She looked so good. You forget how bad coke or smack addicts look until one sobers up. But, man, before she left, she had these deep black circles around her eyes, and was like a hundred pounds. When she came back she was like a buck twenty, or something, she looked great. So I quit too. No program, I just quit. But after that we had to leave Vegas. No way we could make it sober there."

Dolly and Horvath moved to San Francisco in November

1997. There they decided that they would take turns working regular jobs and playing poker. At first Horvath found a position with an accounting firm, while Dolly played about six hours of poker a night at the local card clubs.

> San Fran worked for a while. But we both found out that we were much more addicted to our old lives than we realized. I had the hardest time hearing about poker and not playing, so I quit accounting and started playing again. It was then that I started thinking in a much broader, deeper sense about my attraction to the game. Dolly always said that I was addicted, that I was a compulsive gambler, and maybe looking back now it could seem that way, but I still think of poker as a job. If you take the literal definition of employment, it says something like, The thing at which one works and derives wages. I looked it up once. So I did this thing, and constantly got paid for it. That's a job in my book. It's true that I was jonesing to play when I was working, but what's wrong with loving your job? I missed poker. Not for nothing, but I hate accounting. I hate everything about it. I'm a poker player.

It did not take long for Dolly and Dicky to relapse in other ways as well. Both returned to heroin and cocaine after a few months in San Francisco. "The urge was just too strong," Horvath recollects.

> Right before we started chipping and shooting again, I really felt like we had a chance. Once I came clean and told her I couldn't hold down a regular job anymore, we both kind of broke down. I remember that night so well. We were both so raw. I told her I had to go back to playing poker, and she was totally cool about it. What

we should have done is gotten into rehab again at the same time. If we were both playing poker and getting help, I think we would have been fine. I should have said something that night. I don't know, maybe I was too scared. She would have agreed to it in a heartbeat. I guarantee you. It was such a beautiful night. We were drinking a bottle of wine, sitting out on our stoop. It really hit us that all we had in the world was each other. I told her shit about me that I never told anybody else, and vice versa. I never thought about being married before, but that night, there we were, both sobbing and talking about what we wanted, and I realized all I wanted was her. So I asked her to marry me. And she said yes. Just like that, you know, not even a thought.

Dicky and Dolly married in January 1998 in Reno, and then moved to L.A. "Once we got to southern California, we made all these rules. Only so much poker a week. Only so much smack per day. Those kind of things. But you never keep those rules, you know. You never do. When we hit L.A. we had about ten grand between us. That was our stake, our bankroll. And at first we were both running kind of good. She found a really soft $10–$20 at one of the clubs. And I figured that if we really were going to be poker players, that we have to start taking advantage of every little edge we had."

They began to play as a team. They defined a simple set of signals that they used at the poker tables to inform the other of what card they were holding. This way they could trap players and maximize profitability when they had winning hands. "Playing as a team worked pretty well for a while. We walked into the clubs at different times, started playing different games, and then eventually ended up at the same table. If she had a huge hand she'd stack her chips in a certain way, and I'd know to keep raising so we could make the most out of the hand. Sometimes I would even hit on her like I didn't know her, you know, just to throw people off. It was so sweet."

Like any scam, theirs had its pitfalls.

One day we were at the club by the airport. We had had a huge week, something like eight thousand in the plus column, so we were playing big. It was a $40–$80 table and it was shorthanded, so we kept trapping the same two guys. But in one hand Dolly signaled me that she had pocket aces, there was like five-way action, so I wanted to make sure that there was as much money in the pot as possible. So she raises, the other three guys call and then I raise her. I had some shit hand like four-nine off suit, but I kept raising her to make sure we made the most. I totally missed the flop, but she hit a set, and there was no flush on the board. We knew she was going to win the hand, so I kept betting and raising every chance I had. But when I finally threw my hand in the muck, the cards flipped over and everybody saw them. Everybody knew that something was going on, but nobody could figure out who my partner was. Then one guy noticed that Dolly and I had on identical wedding rings, and that fucked us big time. I never thought about that before, the rings. I guess it was pretty stupid.

The house took our chips and banned us. She went and got the car, and I'm waiting around back when some huge son-of-a-bitch sucker punched me in the back of the head. I think it was a punch, but he could have hit me with a bat for all I know. Dolly found me lying in a pool of blood. He cracked two of my ribs, punctured a lung, and cracked my goddamned skull. But that's the risk you run being a cheat.

After that experience, they never played as a team again.

We kept playing, though. Just not at the same tables. But I still thought that she should take advantage of her looks, you know. I mean a woman as beautiful as Dolly is a total anomaly at a card game. So I told her not to wear her wedding ring at the table anymore, and to dress kind of sexy, but not so sexy that they'd think she was a hooker, just sexy enough that all those guys would think they had a shot with her. I swear, most of these fellas were falling all over themselves to pay her antes and blinds. I don't think she got check-raised once. Eventually she was doing better than I was. But money isn't everything. Giving her that advice was the dumbest thing I ever did. See, we were making money, but we had all these different funds. Let's say I came home after a hundred-dollar win. Twenty-five went to the smack fund, fifty went to food and rent, and the rest would go into our bankroll, to cover our losses if one of us took a bad beat. But that fund thing only worked if we told the truth. I don't know who started lying first, but we both started holding money out of our funds. And once you start lying, well, that's the end of any marriage, isn't it? I'd lie about how much I won so I could pick up extra blow. Then she started holding out cash to buy clothes and stuff. Even though we didn't talk about it, we kind of got used to this frivolous life. And it was fine for a while. We were living two blocks from the beach in Venice. She was even going on a few open auditions. L.A. is a great place when things are going your way. We were just about to make it, that was until I started losing. Poker is lots of things, but more than anything, it's a game of streaks. You get hot, and you think that it's the easiest game in the world. You can't figure out how you ever lost a hand. I had a run where I won thirty nights in a row. It didn't matter if I was getting good cards or shit, I'd hit every flop. But you go cold, and bam, that's the end of everything. It gets so bad that you can't even conceive of a winning situation. I was the first to get cold. One bad beat after another. I'd flop a set of 9s and some tourist would go runner-runner to river a flush. And after a while, Dolly started criticizing my game. She'd watch me play and say that I was too timid, or too aggressive, all that shit. After about a month, money started getting really, really tight. But when you're running bad, there's nothing you can do. I'd play big, small, tight, loose, there was nothing I could do to stop losing. Things got bad enough that I started donating blood and sperm to make extra cash. They'd give me fifty bucks to jerk off in a cup, which isn't that easy when you're high. The heroin and coke kill your sex drive, you know. I felt stupid for wasting my one hard-on of the week on some test tube, but fifty bucks is fifty bucks.

One night I went Hollywood Park to play in a big tournament. And I got crushed. I was the first guy knocked out. So instead of sitting around feeling like a sucker, I jumped in the car and drove right back up to the beach. When I came home there was a BMW in the driveway. And, you know, I knew it right away. I don't know why, but I went in the house anyway. And there was Dolly, getting fucked by some guy on my bed. I was already pretty steamed from the tournament, so after some yelling and throwing some shit, I ended up ramming the guy's car with mine. It's a long story, but he ended up kicking the shit out of me. So that day I caught my wife cheating on me, I wrecked my own car, got my ass kicked, and then spent two days in jail for destruction of private property.

Thing is, that wasn't the end of us. When I got out, Dolly explained that she wasn't cheating on me. She was actually just turning a trick. You know, hooking, 'cause we were so broke. She was at some card table and was getting killed. We were totally broke, and some guy kept hitting on her. She said that she was just doing what I told her to, flirting and such. Then the guy offered her a grand to have sex with him. At first she said no, and then when he went up to two grand she finally gave in. And this is how emotionally fucked up I was, but that kind of made me feel better. You know, like she wasn't cheating or looking for somebody else, we were just broke and she was making a quick buck. She said she was going to split the money with me. So how could I blame her? I got out of jail, into another rehab program, and she swore she'd never turn another trick. But I caught her again like a month later. And a couple of times after that. In 1999 I left L.A. for good. I moved back to New Jersey and started looking for work as an accountant. I tried to get Dolly to come with me. But she stayed in L.A. and kept dealing and auditioning. She said she was clean last I spoke to her. I actually saw her on some sitcom a few months ago. She looked great. I hope she stays that way. I've been a meth addict for about a year now, but it seems easier for some reason this time. Funny thing is, now that I don't gamble or do drugs, I miss the poker a lot more than I do the smack. I wonder what that says about me? I met another woman a few months ago. A lawyer, if you believe that. We were getting pretty close, so I told her my story. She seemed to take it well. She even asked me to teach her how to play poker. Maybe she took it too well.

WHAT CARD DID YOU FOLD AT THE BEGINNING OF THE GAME?

Depend on the rabbit's foot if you will,
but remember, it didn't work for the rabbit.

—ANONYMOUS

There's a guy who lives in Indiana.

One morning he wakes to hear a voice in his head. The voice says, "Quit your job, sell your house, take all your money, and go to Las Vegas."

He ignores the voice and goes to work.

Later in the day, he hears the voice again.

"Quit your job, sell your house, take all your money, and go to Las Vegas."

Again, he ignores the voice.

Soon he hears the voice every minute of the day.

"Quit your job, sell your house, take all your money, and go to Las Vegas."

He can't stand it anymore, so he takes the voice's advice.

He quits his job, sells his house, takes all his money, and flies to Las Vegas.

As soon as he steps off the plane, the voice says, "Go to Binion's Horseshoe."

He goes to the Horseshoe.

The voice says, "Buy an entry into the World Series of Poker."

He puts up his $10,000 and buys a seat in the tournament.

He goes to his assigned table.

In his first hand the guy is dealt A♠ A♣ .

The voice says, "Go all in."

He pushes his entire $10,000 bankroll into the pot.

Three players call.

The dealer lays down the flop: 9♥ 10♥ J♥ .

The voice says, "Fuck."

Without turning back to the previous page, answer the following questions:

1. How many times did the voice say "Quit your job, sell your house, take all your money, and go to Las Vegas?"
2. What was the player dealt?
3. What was the flop?
4. Where was the guy from?
5. How much money did he bet on the one hand?

It doesn't really matter if you can answer all those questions. If you are like most people, the mechanism that is your memory—why and when and how you recall things—is a total mystery to you. You might remember the hand but not the fact that the guy was from Indiana. You might even recollect what song was playing when you lost your virginity, but not the song that was on the radio when you woke up this morning. The point is that human memory is an imperfect and bizarre phenomenon. It also happens to be one of the only attributes of poker excellence that can be improved while you are away from the table.

There are lots of different ways to learn the game of poker. I've found that no matter how unique or innovative the technique was by which you learned the game, it probably fit neatly into one of two categories: smart or dumb.

The only genuinely intelligent method is to learn the way Richard Nixon did. Born as a devoted Quaker, Nixon managed to remain unfamiliar with any form of gambling until his mid-twenties, when he joined the United States Navy during the early years of World War II. That's where he got his first exposure to poker. It intrigued him from the start. After watching the game for a while, he approached a fellow officer who played regularly with a question. He wanted to know if there was any sure way to win at poker. Eventually, the officer told him, and went on to explain the most fundamental notions of the game.

Nixon took great interest and played heads-up with his friend for months for no money. Before he was willing to risk a penny, Nixon got tons of experience under his belt. He went on to be such an efficient player that he partially funded his first senate run with proceeds from his poker winnings.

I, on the other hand, approached the game with no such reverence. Suffering from what Greek philosophers called hubris, I jumped right into any poker game I could, even though I was usually completely overmatched. If I won, I thought it was because of my superior skill. When I lost, I thought that I just got unlucky. It, of course, was the other way around.

I began to play regularly in casino games in early 1991. That's when I started to suspect that I wasn't the best poker player on the planet. I was getting killed on a regular basis. Being dumb and arrogant, I kept returning to the tables where I was getting beat. And after getting crushed for a few months, I started to develop a strange and alien personality trait: humility.

I went to my poker mentor and asked how I could improve my game. He told me that there were three ways that I could improve my skills: learn the odds, play more poker, and most importantly, improve my memory. "A good memory is the one thing that all great card players have in common," he said.

That was an extremely frustrating concept to me. Part of my attraction to poker was that it seemed to be a purely equal-opportunity endeavor. Most of the competitive activities I undertook in my athletic career were uphill fights. The two varsity sports I played in college were volleyball and lacrosse. In both games height and girth were very important. I had neither. So I had to work twice as hard to be effective. I hated the idea that certain people were blessed with great memories, and again, I'd have to struggle to catch up.

When I expressed my dissatisfaction with this revelation to the professor, he told me that nothing could be further from the truth. "You're not born with a great memory," he said. "You make one."

"What about somebody like Stu Unger?" I asked. If there ever was a poker player with a perfect memory, it was Stu Unger.

"Unger? He was going to be the example I used to show how

memory is an acquired trait." Then he went on to explain himself. Stu never really went to school, and he spent most of his formative years hanging out with degenerates, mobsters, and gamblers. And regardless of this intellectually deprived adolescence, Stu developed what he called "total recall." He didn't even appreciate his skill. He thought remembering everything was a "pain in the ass."

Stu and Victor Romano, a hit man for the Genovese crime family of New York, used to get together periodically to go over every hand of gin each had played that week. They dealt them out from memory. Romano was also said to have total recall. The professor told me that Romano had memorized the entire Webster's dictionary and could recite the definition of any word contained within.

As far as I was concerned, such staggering intellectual capacity, created from such an uninspiring environment, had to be a genetic gift. That's where I was wrong. In reality, every aspect of Stu's childhood was an asset to creating an amazing memory, not a hindrance.

Stu grew up in New York in the early 1960s. It was before OTB, gambling in Atlantic City, or even Lotto, so every bar on every city block had a local bookie. Stu's father, Isadore Unger, was the shylock for a dive bar on lower Second Avenue. Though Isadore wanted Stu to grow up to be a doctor or lawyer, he used to take Stu into the bar frequently.

Stu ended up picking up a lot of information while in the bar. By the time he was seven, he was secretly studying his father's business. Isadore would write down bets, and Stu, not wanting to get caught, would memorize winning numbers, horse race results, anything that he could get his hands on. He loved his father's life.

Wanting to get Stu away from the bar and New York City, Isadore would send the family up to the Catskill Mountains every summer. That way Stu would be able to run around, swim, and make friends with other nice Jewish kids. Stu ended up spending most of his time looking over his mother's shoulder while she was playing gin. Stu caught on to the game right away. It was as easy as memorizing numbers. Within a few months his understanding of the game exceeded hers. He began to correct her mistakes when he was eight. Before long he was playing the hotel staff for their paychecks. He started to see cards as a way to avoid the thing he hated more than anything: school.

All of those factors led to Unger's genius. He wasn't born with an innate ability to remember cards; he learned it from studying his father's business and watching his mother play gin. And most importantly, he loved the topic. Though he might not have known the names of the techniques he used, there's no doubt that Unger unwittingly employed tricks like coding, chunking, and mnemonics.

That justified the existence of Unger's memory to me, but then I asked the professor about Stu's accomplice, Victor Romano. He was an uneducated soldier for one of the New York crime families. How in the world could he have memorized the entire dictionary unless he was born with a great memory?

The professor laughed. "You know where Romano learned to do that trick with the dictionary? He was serving a three-to-six sentence in the Attica penitentiary. Even a dog could memorize the dictionary given three years."

Well, maybe not *my* dog. But I did see his point.

It turns out that everything I knew, or thought I knew rather, about the human memory has been a misconception. Memory isn't a section of the brain. It's not a tangible thing. It is more like a process or series of processes that take place all over the brain. And the worst part, or perhaps the best, is the fact that there is no secret trick to acquiring a great memory.

The most common fallacy is the notion that there is such a thing as a photographic memory. People assume that certain individuals are actually capable of storing a literal image in their heads and then reproducing the facts contained within at any moment. Chess masters have been the group most associated with photographic memories. Any one of them would need only about thirty seconds to memorize the position of pieces on a chessboard to be able to reproduce them moments later. Most memory experts assumed that they would take a mental picture of the board and then could reproduce it accordingly. This turns out not to be the case. These masters were only able to complete the task when the board made sense to them; if the pieces were distributed in accordance with the rules of chess. When the pieces were placed randomly on the board, with no care given to their chess propertics, the master couldn't recall where the pieces were on the board, even after memorizing it for twenty minutes. Some went as far as to say that the random board was actually hard to look at. One even said it hurt.

Other evidence that would contradict the existence of a photographic memory was obtained by asking memory subjects to memorize a chart of numbers like the one below.

3	1	0	4	4	9	9	1
0	0	1	2	1	9	7	6
1	0	0	6	7	8	5	4
3	6	8	6	4	8	0	8
6	3	6	7	8	7	6	8
7	6	4	3	1	1	1	0
9	8	6	5	4	7	8	9
7	6	5	6	5	4	4	6

Subjects were given a few minutes to study the sixty-four

numbers on the chart and then asked to reproduce them. Most subjects were successful in their ability to quickly re-create the series of numbers, reciting them one after another. But when they were asked what the first number in the last row was, it took them more time to figure out. That was because they did not have an image of the grid in their heads, but rather had to count out to the fifty-sixth digit as they had memorized them in order.

Okay, so they are not taking a metal image of the chart. But still, how is anyone capable of memorizing so many numbers? The first trick to memorizing something like the chart above is known as coding.

The process of coding is essential to memory. If a person is asked to remember eleven random digits, they will have a tough time recalling them at a later date; 15557694086 is a hard thing to remember. But code it in some way, break it up, and it becomes much more manageable: 1-555-769-4086. That's what the dashes and spaces in phone numbers and social security numbers are there for.

If you were asked to recall the first two lines of the chart (3104499100121976), it would be almost impossible to do without coding or breaking up the number in some way. Try it. Now break it up into some format that makes sense to you: 310 is an L.A. area code; 44 was Reggie Jackson's number; 99 was Wayne Gretzsky's; 10012 is some New York zip code; and 1976 was the year of the American bicentennial. Much easier to do it that way.

Another strategy similar to coding can be used if you're trying to remember the up cards a person has folded in a game of seven-card stud. If one of your opponents gets dealt his fourth up card (his hand looks like [K♥][10♦][J♥][3♣]) and then folds after a bet, an easy way to recall what cards he had is to make a story or mnemonic out of them. The story for the hand could sound something like: The romantic king had ten rich kids who looked like him and liked to stay out until three in the morning clubbing. It's often easier to remember words that make sense than numbers that do not.

Some mnemonic strategy is based on the fact that there are two kinds of memory, short-term and long-term. Long-term memory is used to store things over a lifetime—your seventh birthday party, your mother's maiden name, that sort of thing. Long-term memory seems to have an almost unlimited capacity. Short-term memory, however, is very limited indeed.

The average human being can hold only about six or seven items in his mind simultaneously. After that, the brain starts to discard old memories to make room for new ones. That's where a technique called chunking comes in. If you had to remember the letters F-U-L-L-H-O-U-S-E individually, you might have a tough time. But chunk them all together, and "full house" isn't so tough to keep in mind.

Many other factors make it easier for an individual to learn or memorize something. How meaningful the subject is to that person is very important. Chess masters have a much easier time memorizing concepts related to chess. Also, the ability to associate a subject with something you're already familiar with helps. Students across America find the easiest state to recognize is Michigan. This is because they know it looks like a mitten. I'm not even sure where Idaho is, let alone what it looks like.

A great memory is a huge asset at a card table for a number of reasons. The ability to store information and recall it at any time goes far beyond some simple skill like counting cards (although remembering in a game of seven-card stud that five hearts have been burned, and then being able to recalculate the odds of drawing your fifth heart to make the flush is a huge asset). But more than that, there is the capability of recalling specific situations. With the wealth of empirical wisdom to draw from, you become a much more efficient player. You can begin to predict human nature. You can remember the exact card transactions that have taken place in similar situations. Or even better, you can create a book on a specific player.

There's lots of down time at a poker table, time between hands or waiting for slower players to make up their minds. To fill those gaps, certain players just love to talk. This wouldn't be so bad if they didn't, nine out of ten times, say the exact same things over and over again. In Texas Hold'em, when two guys show the same hand—say, if they both play queen-10—after they've showed their hands, one will undoubtedly look at the other and say, "You play that shit?" Or if somebody misdeals, some idiot will always say, "Hey, we ain't playing 52 pickup." Hearing the same expressions over and over again always makes me picture my own personal poker doll. Like one of those little baby figurines that has a string on it and when the string is pulled some cute pearl will come out of its mouth, like "Mama." Only mine would be of a heavyset man in a jogging suit that says things like "Chop it up!" "You play that shit?" or "Deal the fucking cards!"

Bobby Greene loves to chat it up at a poker table. To his credit, the things that come out of his mouth are often witty or insightful, but still he does talk far too much during a game. What he does more than anything is dabble in theoretical poker. A hand rarely goes by without his telling you what he folded. This isn't as much annoying as it is detrimental . . . to him. If you can remember the information Robert freely disperses, it is very easy to make a book on him.

The first thing you can figure out is what starting hands he likes. After listening to him talk (which I have been doing since the Iran-Contra hearings were in session), any person can start to deduce what kind of hands he will and won't play in different situations.

Also, in talking about his folded hand, Bobby lets me know what kind of drawing hand he will abandon and when. A player who tells you what his hand was makes it easy to figure out if he's calculating pot odds or not. If he is (Bobby does), then I can figure out how much to bet to keep him in or make him fold, depending on what I'm holding in my hand.

The other thing you can know about people who chat during a poker game, is that by talking so much, they're announcing that they're not creating a book on you. You're ahead of the game.

The most common association people have with memory and cards is professional blackjack players called card counters. These people have Rainman-like abilities to memorize the position of the 416 cards in an eight-deck shoe. There are only a handful of people on the planet who can perform such a feat. They are known throughout the gambling community and are banned from almost all games in a casino, for good reason.

In a game of blackjack the house has roughly a 2 percent edge over the player, which means that for every $100 wagered, the house has an expected return of $2. But when a card counter employs his skills and recalculates the odds of drawing to certain cards after he has seen a fair portion of the shoe pass by, he can turn the tables on the casinos and generate a 1 to 5 percent edge—in some extreme cases even more. That's why casinos ban known card counters from playing. In the long run, probability theory says that these people will take money from the house. But it's not a sure thing. Remember, the counter has to work very, very hard to get that edge, and even then there's a chance that he will lose.

There are a number of different card-counting strategies in blackjack. Team play is perhaps the most common. The year after I left graduate school and began to play a lot of poker, I met a group of young cardplayers. There were four of them, all in their mid-twenties and, like myself, coming out of some unsatisfactory employment experience. They lived in New York but would travel almost anywhere to play in a lively poker game where no one knew them, and therefore, they could gain an advantage by cheating or playing as a team.

The four of them—Will, Ben, Harsh (that was really his name), and Adam—were young enough and unassuming enough to blend into any card game without coming off as pros (I always laugh when I see some guy at a table with a fedora hat and shades, introducing himself as "Chicago" or "Crusher." Who the hell is going to want to play with that guy?).

Will and Adam had both gone to fancy Ivy League schools. Ben used to work at a big-time brokerage house in New York, and Harsh was an MIT grad school dropout. They looked like nice clean-cut kids, and they intended to. Anonymity was an important part of their plan. Between scamming a few home games and grinding out small wins in the poker houses, they were each clearing about $35,000 to $40,000 a year after taxes (meaning no taxes).

All four of these guys were remarkably intelligent, and if they had put a quarter of the effort they put into cards into anything else, they would have undoubtedly been wildly successful. But they chose the road less traveled: to quote Harsh, "Working sucks." How they didn't see sitting on their asses drinking awful coffee for marathon ten-hour card sessions in smoke-filled basements as work, I have no idea.

I began to see them around the card clubs and casinos enough to become friendly with them. One day Harsh approached me with a proposition. All four of them had been learning to count cards. Each had gotten to the point of being able to count well over four decks, which for blackjack purposes was plenty. Plus, you never really need to know exactly what cards have gone by and in what order, you just need to know percentages. They had formed a blackjack cartel and wanted me to join. At the time I could only count one deck (which I can't even do anymore), so I pointed out that I wouldn't be much use to them. Harsh told me that I didn't need to count, that I was going to be their "big player." After he explained the scam to me, I agreed to join in.

Our cartel operated like this: Five guys walk into a casino in Atlantic City. Four of them have $1,000 each in their wallets. The fifth—that was me—has thirty grand stuffed into his pocket. The four "LPs" (little players) each find a centrally located, low-level blackjack table ($10 minimum wager, $1,000 maximum) to play at. The big player (me), with a rack containing thirty grand in chips sitting in front of him, would hang out at the bar and hit on waitresses. It was very important that all four LPs were visible from where I was sitting. We went to four casinos before we found one with a suitable layout.

Now the scam begins. Each LP plays blackjack at his own table and counts cards. Like I said, they're not remembering how many 6s of spades have passed, they are just retaining as much information about the shoe as possible that is relevant to our intention. All we are looking for is what's called a "friendly deck," one that is heavy in aces and 10s (meaning face cards also). That way the deck becomes a lot more predictable.

In a normal deck, cards valued at 10 and aces make up 38 percent of the cards. We were looking for a shoe somewhere in the neighborhood of 42 or 43 percent, meaning that out of the first hundred cards going by, we needed about eighty to be non-premium cards. It takes an anomalous distribution of cards to stack the deck like that, but that kind of thing happens every day.

This way, the dealer's up card reveals more about his hand

than usual. Having a 6 up is more likely to result in a bust than with a normal deck that isn't friendly. Another advantage is that the odds of getting a blackjack—which pays the player 3-2 on his wager—have turned in our favor. Our cartel is also able to use splitting rules to our advantage as well.

A player who is dealt to cards of equal value—two 8s, for example, or a 10 and a king—is able to make two separate hands out of them, and therefore double his bet. The standard blackjack thinking is, Never split a winner. You've got twenty and the dealer has a 6 showing, don't get greedy, just take your winnings and be happy. But now we know that the deck is stacked toward big cards. This allows us to be more liberal with splitting and doubling because the outcome is more predictable. When we split our 8s against his 5, we are more likely to get the big cards we need to get to eighteen, and he is also more likely to bust.

Each LP sits and bets the table minimum, biding his time until the deck falls in our favor. So I sit at the bar and look the part of some drunk rich kid from New York (I do that really well) with thirty g's in front of me. All the time I'm watching my four friends, waiting for the signal. As soon as one of them stands up and stretches, I come running over to the table and play as many hands as I can at the highest limit until the shoe runs out. Then I go back to the bar.

We ran this scam three times in about a year. The first time we won nine grand, the second we won seven, and the last time we dropped $20,000 in five minutes.

When we left, those guys looked like they'd been carrying bricks or cleaning toilets for a month. For all the numbers and statistics crammed into their heads, for all the cards they'd memorized over the year, I doubt they remember anything as well as they remember driving home $20,000 in the hole. That's the funny thing about pro gamblers; when you do the math, Will and Harsh making forty g's a year, it's like getting paid in the neighborhood of $25 an hour.

SEX, LIES, AND A DECK OF CARDS

In the last couple of weeks I have seen the ads for the Wonder Bra. Is that really a problem in this country? Men not paying enough attention to women's breasts?

—HUGH GRANT

I've had friends tell me that their sex lives were completely dependent on how they fared in a game of poker, that their poor wives or girlfriends stay up till two in the morning, watching TV, pacing the house, waiting up to see if they won. If they did, fantastic, let the real games begin. They'd be up for a couple more hours. If not, well, okay, at least there was a good night's sleep to look forward to.

One such acquaintance describes a poker room as the most sexually charged atmosphere in the world. Hmmm, let me think about that for a second. Ten people are crammed around a table.

A space of about two inches separates their elbows. Nobody has moved in hours. The room is stuffy and stale, yet many of them smoke. They cough without covering their mouths. One or two have not bathed in days. Everybody's hands are covered with a thin black film from fondling bacterially unsound chips and cards. The guy eating the fajita is dripping hot sauce on the green felt. Nope, sexy doesn't really leap to mind. But, I will admit that somehow, through all of this behavior that is at the very least unattractive, and at the worst a biohazard, sex and gender does play a huge role in poker.

The most obvious sexual impact of the game is on what I call "mixed" couples. By mixed, I mean a union of loving individuals containing one normal person and one degenerate gambler. The effect poker has on these couples is vast, thorough, and undeniable. To be more specific, it has ruined every relationship I've ever had in my life but one.

I could whine about the difficulties inherent in modern romance. I could claim to be misunderstood. But honestly, I suspect that coming home at four in the morning smelling of booze and cigarettes, with a couple of thousand dollars less in my pocket than I left the house with, just ain't good for a relationship.

Also, I'm starting to think that the company I keep is a substantial pitfall. That's because a large number of the poker players I know are what one ex used to call "people of salacious character." I'd go out with some of the guys from the club for a din-ner with the most innocuous intentions. I'd hope we'd talk about the stock market or perhaps life as it's seen from our unique per-spective, but invariably a card game would break out, and then a few hours later we'd end up at some strip joint or massage parlor.

Take that, and couple it with the fact that for most of my early twenties I was nothing more than a grab bag of various insecuri-ties and emotional afflictions, and you end up with the series of comically failed relationships that I have experienced. To make things worse, when I'd run across relationship difficulties, I often turned to those people from the club for advice. Who could for-get such pearls of wisdom as, "Women are the rake of life," or "If she doesn't get you, three to one she's a dyke anyway."

My thrice-divorced thirty-five-year-old friend Max once said, "Why is it that they always expect us to change? How about them changing for once?" Right. Now if I could only get these wonderful women to stop patiently waiting at home, taking care of my dog while I gamble our futures away, then I'd really be on to something.

All of my relationships play out with an almost formulaic pre-dictability. There is a honeymoon period, of course, where all the poker-related trappings seem romantic and original to my girl-friend. Cardplayers are many terrible things, but one thing we're not is ordinary. We keep our own hours, we have no boss or reg-

imented existence. To the untrained eye, it looks like the life of
Riley. Even the card club itself and the mobsterlike guys that fill
it have, at first glance, a curious appeal.

I've spent years trying to anatomize the origin of that initial
bliss, and I hate to say this, but I've found that a large part of it is
the money. Not that any of the women I've dated were gold dig-
gers (if they were, they were digging in the wrong place), but
poker players just have an unusual way of dealing with finances.
We're just more carefree about it than most people are. When
somebody who knows little about the lifestyle is exposed to it, a
poker player's lack of concern for the big picture, for things like
savings or mortgages, can look spontaneous and sexy.

That is, of course, all an illusion. Most gamblers I know are
almost always broke. The catch is, we're the only ones who are
aware of that. To the rest of the world, we look like Rockefellers.
Who else walks around with four grand cash in their pockets? We
do it because we have to. Either we need the money to play with
or, like Stu Unger, we're just so baffled by the notion of a checking account that we keep every penny we have in our pockets. A
normal human being is only going to have that much cash on
them if they're going to buy a jet-ski.

Poker players are like conduits for money. In any one year I
may handle one million different dollars, but that's just because
I'm constantly winning and losing. I'm certainly not putting any-

thing away. And that transience has an effect. It leads to something I call the paradox of profligacy. In short, I've become very used to parting with money. If I lose a thousand-dollar pot on the river because some idiot hit his only out in the deck, it's happened to me so many times that I swear, I won't even blink. Sure that extra grand would have been nice. But big deal, there's a good chance I would have lost it on the next hand anyway.

This makes me the perfect pigeon for salesmen. When I rent a car, I've made it a policy to always price the cheapest model. But somehow that rental agent knows it's me on the other end of the line, and points out that the convertible is only thirty dollars a day more. Thirty bucks? Come on, what's thirty bucks to a man as dumb as I am? That's a penny ante hand of poker. *Voilà*, I'm driving a convertible. It's like I can't help but look as if I am a big spender even though I am usually one bad night away from an extended stay in the poker hospital.

That's the catch. The luster of this life comes off pretty fast. The petty crooks around the poker scene that appear so sexy at first glance are, in actuality, nothing more than the low-level criminals they turn out to be. It's nice to know a guy named Tips Tripoli, but once you find out that he got his moniker because he's a pickpocket, and every time he bumps into you, you have to grab for your wallet, it gets old very quickly. The same thing is true for all the high rollers that hang around the poker club. From afar their lives seem enviable, but after knowing them for about a week, you see them as nothing more than the degenerate gamblers that they are. It usually takes about three months for a woman to figure all that out about me, for the fascination with the lifestyle to fade, and then the honeymoon ends and she walks out. Some have run.

I've culled what I believe to be a universal truth from all of my failed relationships and the explanations (lies) and apologies (groveling) contained within them. Ready? Here it is: There is a big difference between men and women. There, I said it. But I'm not just talking the stuff I learned in sex ed—the anatomical things—the difference I'm speaking of is specifically the capacity of the genders to accept and appreciate concepts such as poker and gambling.

In the late 1980s I read a poker book by man named David Spanier. Within those pages I found the rhetoric necessary to construct a purely sexist creed. Spanier wrote, "The *machismo* of poker is significant. It is the characteristic of the game. Both sexes play bridge together; among gambling games, both sexes play blackjack, roulette, or baccarat without any special attention being accorded to women; craps, with its noise and go-go atmosphere, is somewhat more of a male preserve. But poker, preeminently, is a man's game. Not that woman are excluded, but the virtues of successful poker, which have colored the game since its earliest days, are the swashbuckling male qualities of courage, aggression, and bluff."

Narrow-minded as that all may seem now, that sexist thesis stood as my creed for many years. For most of my youth I was an outspoken proponent of this theory, single-handedly keeping alive a philosophy dead long before I was born. Then I met a beautiful twenty-six-year-old Russian woman named Yana Andropov. Our introduction was a watershed event for me—one that triggered a rapid deterioration of my philosophies. In a sense, she did to me what glasnost did to the Union of Soviet Socialist Republics.

Yana was a refugee from a small town on the Kamchatka Peninsula called Magadan. Four years before I met her, Yana had left home to avoid continuous sexual advances from her stepfather. To escape, she literally stowed away on a Swedish-registered freighter bound for Tokyo. There she met a Japanese party promoter named Takashi. She worked in his nightclub for almost a month, but quit immediately after she thinks he slipped a hit of Rohypnol into her drink and molested her. That's when she hopped aboard a Nippon Air flight to New York.

I include all of these details when reciting Yana's story because I remember each and every one very clearly. People say that the mark of a good con is in the details.

When she arrived in New York in 1995, Yana started waitressing at one of the Russian poker clubs in Queens. I know waiting tables is no picnic; I've done it, it sucks. But tending to cardplayers at a club is not a tough job at all for the women who do it. In fact, as long as you don't mind an old man's hand on your ass every once in a while, it's got to be one of the easiest gigs in the world. There are only about four things on the menu, there are no complicated drink orders to remember, you just have to smile, giggle, and wink every once in a while. On any given night, there is some lonely old man winning thousands of dollars who is looking to act like a big shot. The friendlier waitresses make around $500 a night.

Yana was born for the work. There wasn't one second of her waking day that she wasn't trying to get something from somebody. She told me her entire life's story the first night we met while I was waiting for my Hold'em game to start. I remember being moved by the details. Two days later, she pulled me aside and told me that she had a dream about me—a complicated, highly symbolic dream with none-too-subtle sexual overtones. Two days after that she woke up in my bed.

It was a very short-lived relationship—three days, two nights. In hindsight, I wonder what took so long. On the third morning I woke up, and Yana was gone. So was the only expensive thing I've ever owned, my Rolex. It had vanished off my night table. Of course she took it. That wasn't the mystery. I was just curious about where she was headed. L.A., Vegas, back to Russia, who knew? One thing I was pretty sure of was that I'd never see her again. After all, you don't rip off somebody who hangs out in the same circle as you except as a departing gesture. Card clubs are filled with stories of people who loaned somebody they'd known for years a bunch of money, and then never saw them again. In fact Korean Rich did that to me, among others, his last night in New York. He ran around the club, quietly borrowing as much as he could from all of his friends, and then left town.

The funny thing is that nobody really disappears. Somebody always knows somebody who was on vacation in New Mexico and saw Korean Rich in a card club near Albuquerque. I assumed that I'd hear about Yana at some point a few years down the line.

I chalked up my interaction with her as a learning experience and tried to keep her—and my Rolex—out of my mind. As usual, I went to Winchester that night to play in my friendly $10–$20 game. I cut the deck, dealt the cards, looked up, and saw that Yana was seated at my table. She smiled at me.

I assumed that as soon as I asked her about my watch, she'd get angry and act insulted. Maybe throw in a "How dare you?" followed by a couple of well-chosen Russian insults. That's what anybody else would do, particularly a poker player. She was, after all, just running a bluff. So I went through the motions and asked.

"Um . . . I don't think so," she said. Then she smiled, kissed me, and asked if she could come over later that night. Even though the only other thing of value in my house was my dog (and I don't know how much she could get for a used Newfoundland), I still said I was busy.

What I quickly learned about her was that she wasn't looking to pull a Korean Rich. My watch wasn't a door prize. It turns out that Yana was a poker player, just like me. She was just looking to get some startup money. She hated waiting tables. Instead of hustling the guys at the club with a tray in her hand, she wanted to do it with a deck of cards. All she needed was one idiot to give her an opportunity at some decent seed money, and she'd be on her way. And in a room filled with bozos, dopes, yahoos, and morons, I was the guy she thought would be the easiest to take. Talk about being the last kid picked in a kickball game.

I see Yana around the clubs all the time. She's caught in a very predictable poker pattern. When she's running well she plays in big games, when she's not she moves down to the $10–$20. I see that kind of thing a lot, and it's very unproductive. Just because you can beat one game doesn't mean you can beat the others. Playing over your head is the classic mistake a low-level player can make. Winning players stay right where they are. That's the way to make money at poker. If you can crush a game, stay there until the well runs dry. Only gamblers try to move up to bigger games. They do it for the fix instead of the money, and that's usually the end of them.

Periodically, Yana will show up at the club with a very conservative-looking guy, some Wall Street type who at first thought it was a huge turn-on to have a poker-playing girlfriend. He'll stay for a bit, watch her play a hand or two, and then head off. She stays till the club closes at dawn. During the games Yana complains about how the guy doesn't understand her lifestyle and how they are about to break up because of all of his nagging.

She dated a friend of mine named Jelly for a little while. After they broke up, Jelly confided in me that the reason the relationship ended was that he couldn't take her coming home at five in the morning, drunk and broke, anymore. That's when I started to think that David Spanier's sexist credo might be wrong.

First of all, Yana is not a grifter. She may run some scams, but that is not her profession of choice. The cons are just a means to an end. She's just trying to make enough money out of them to be a poker player. And everything in the world around her—friends, men, women, money, sleep, sex—is secondary to that pursuit. In short, she's just like every male poker player I know.

When she first started to play regularly, nobody really took her that seriously. She was almost always the only woman at the table. She was a novelty, a distraction. But the fact is, my personal feelings for her aside, she has become an excellent low-limit poker player. That revelation stood in defiance of everything I thought I had learned about the sexes. Having never dated a man, I always assumed that the difficulties inherent in my relationships were due to the differences between men and women. But having known Yana over the years, and also a number of other women who started to play at the clubs after her, I've begun to think that the problems I experience with women are not due to the asymmetry in the yin and the yang, but those existing between sickness and sanity. I now believe that all poker junkies are alike—man, woman, or child, it does not matter.

Every year more women learn to play the game. And every year, those who play learn to play it better. And still, the notion of gender equality in poker is far from accepted. No matter how skilled or successful she is, a female player is often looked down upon. In fact, among the many different tournaments offered during the World Series of Poker, there is an all-women's Hold'em tournament. I asked one of the WSOP coordinators why they offer a separate game when women are allowed to participate in the main tournament. He replied, "So they'll have a chance to win something. You got to keep the boys and girls apart for it to be fair."

When an event such as the U.S. Open Tennis tournament separates the competitor by sex, that I get. I don't think anybody can argue that there are not physical differences between men and women. But why, in an event like the World Series of Poker, are there distinctions made between men and women? Brute strength is not an asset. If anything, the archetypal attributes possessed by women—intuitiveness, thoughtfulness, and cunning—would make them better at poker than men. For some reason, most believe that this is not the case. And in all the years the World Series of Poker has been held, no woman has won the main event.

World Series champion Huck Seed once said, "I understand why men run faster than women, it's an evolutionary thing, but in poker . . . I'd rather not talk about that." Other pros are more outspoken. One of the senior members of the professional ranks is Amarillo Slim Preston, a seventy-something native of Texas who still wears a cowboy hat and a bolo tie to play. A few years ago he was asked about how he felt playing in the World Series with so many women. Slim replied, "Women are meant to be loved and not play poker. My wife Helen Elizabeth thinks that a king is a ruler of a country and a queen is his bedmate. A woman would have a better chance of putting a wildcat in a tobacco sack than she would of coming out to Vegas and beating me."

The year 2000 was a breakthrough year for women at the World Series. Jerri Thomas won the third event of the WSOP, a $1,500 buy-in seven-card stud tournament that had 245 mostly male entrants. Her first prize was worth $135,975. Melissa Hayden came in second in the $5,000 buy-in limit Hold'em tournament, and Annie Duke came in tenth in the main event.

Melissa Hayden admits that there is still plenty of sexism in poker.

> I think there's still some sexism at the table, but nothing like it used to be. It's even come a long way since I started to play in big games a few years ago. I used to get a lot of, "How does somebody like *you* learn the game?" I've always hated that question. The way they ask it makes me sound like a jockey trying out for the NBA or something like that. How does somebody like *me* learn the game? I picked it up the usual way: from my dad when I was a kid. I started to play a little more regularly when I dated a poker player in college. Then, when I moved to New York, I formed a regular game with some friends at my old job. It's not like I'm a one-armed wrestler, or even a Hebrew Jesus scholar. I'm just a woman who makes her living playing cards.

Melissa used to design book covers for a major publishing house in New York City. She gave up full-time work of any kind in 1997 to play poker. "The more I learned about the game, the more that I was exposed to it, the more I was convinced that I could play for a living. The funny thing is that I didn't approach it as 'Could I, a woman, play poker professionally.' I only wondered if I, as Melissa, could do it. And it looks like I can. . . . I've heard that Amarillo Slim quote. But he's not like that anymore. He's lost a few hands to some women over the years. Occasionally,

Slim comes by a table I'm playing and warns the men that they're in deep trouble. It's kind of a nice feeling, to win the respect of those amazing players. And it's a better feeling when I beat them."

Melissa thinks that all of these sexist prejudices will shortly be a thing of the past.

> Our situation as female poker players isn't really similar to something like suffragettism, where women have to march and picket and fight for equality and recognition. In poker, more and more woman are playing the game. And there isn't anything anybody can do to stop it. Not like they'd want to. But right now, if you look at the number of female participants in relation to the number of men, the tournament results are just about in line with what you'd expect. But as more women take to the game, then the tournament wins by women will go up as well. It's only a matter of time before women start winning the big games with regularity. Recognizing woman as equals, or even superiors, isn't something that we've all got to pitch in and fight for, it's kind of more like an inevitability.

Angelica Stark, another professional player, goes beyond aspiring to gender equality. She assumes that eventually women are going to be better than men on a lot of the games. "Listen, there are differences between the sexes. You can't deny that. And there are times where men are better equipped for a specific job. You need somebody to carry a sofa up a set of stairs, that's a man's work. You need something blown up? I'd say that's another good one. Hey, they just have skills in areas that we don't. I'm okay with that. But then, you've got to admit that men aren't as . . . you know, sharp as us. I ought to know."

Even though she is twenty-nine, Angelica had been living with her father and three brothers up until a year ago. "I saw the best and worst of the male of the species every day." To provide her with further insight, when the cards aren't running well, she is an employee of a very well respected Vegas hotel as a masseuse.

First of all, fifty percent of my massages are, you know, regular. For those I get seventy-five dollars an hour, plus tip. Depending on the guy, I charge twenty-five to one hundred extra for what we call massage with release. But the great thing is that after the guy is finished, he's finished, you know, totally done. He doesn't want to be massaged anymore. So, about ten minutes into the massage, I kind of work near the area to see if the guy is up for the special treatment. I'd guess that probably two out of three are. No joke. A lot aren't even interested when they first come in, but about twenty minutes in I start doing my special thing, and of course the guy doesn't want me to stop. It's almost too easy. I start doing the thing and get him to the point that he thinks I'm going to finish it, and then I quote the price. No shit, I could say name your firstborn after me and the guy would agree. So I finish, and then he wants me to go. So sometimes I'll get one-fifty or two hundred dollars for twenty-five minutes' work.

Men are just like that. They're like these giant walking swollen glands. They can't help themselves. I've had the most faithful men on my table, who turn down the massage with release like ten times before we start, "Just a straight massage, please. No funny business." And as soon as I put one finger near his little friend, he acts like he's got no choice but to beg for it. They are cattle. It's the same thing with poker. Every guy plays like he's hard up with a hard-on. I've seem them do the stupidest things at a poker table. They are just too pigheaded to think that anybody ever has them beat. Woman are more clearheaded. They think about stuff before they act. You don't see bunches of girls lining up to pay me hundreds of dollars to do something to them that they could do better themselves for free. I mean, I know what I'm doing and all, but it is his dick. What does he need me for? That's where the difference is going to be at the poker tables. I think you're gonna find that the more scientific games like stud are going to be dominated by men, where the sexier, more passionate games like Hold'em are going to belong to the women. Take somebody like Huck Seed. He's super at any game of cards. But the first thing his girlfriend picked up was Hold'em. She's only been playing a little while, and she's already super too. I'll bet that in a year or two she'll be better than him. And you know what, it'll be great for their relationship. Talk about sexual energy. I've never been so turned on as when I first played a guy I was dating heads-up. Remember, the family that plays together, stays together.

I wish I had interviewed her sooner.

THE HOUSE OF CARDS

I've spent so much time in casinos that if you put a
coin in my mouth and pulled my arm,
my eyes would spin.

—JESSE MAY,
novelist and poker writer

For as long as it's been illegal, there's been poker played in New York City. My father told me about going to a dingy card room in Greenwich Village in the late 1950s. If you overlook his use of the words *greasers* or *hip cats,* his description of the club was very similar to the ones that I regular these days. Basically, all you need to make a club is a roof, a deck of cards, and a table. Getting the players is the least of your worries. They'll find the club, no matter where it is. Poker is often a very desperate hobby.

Nowadays, there are tons of poker rooms operating in the five boroughs. Each has its own unique appeal and drawback. Some are safer than others. Some are more colorful. But no matter how different they are, there is one thing that unifies them all. In a room where every individual is technically breaking the law, no one involved acts like they are doing anything wrong or out of the ordinary.

I remember going to the Winchester for the first time in 1995. I expected it to have a secluded entrance. Perhaps I'd have to say something like *"the blue calf crosses at midnight"* to a heavily tattooed man in a tank top guarding the door. Of course there was nothing like that. The Winchester was located in the basement of a high-rise residential building. You just walked through some glass doors, down some stairs, knocked on another door, and you'd be in. You could get the Winchester's phone number by calling information or looking up poker on the Internet.

The ambience is very similar to any corner bar. It's a little dingy, you feel a little guilty for being there, but it's nice to fit in and know the regulars. It's a little like *Cheers,* where not only does everybody know your name, but they know your business as well. A poker table is worse than a sewing circle. Everybody knows how everybody else is running. They know who's up, who's down, and whose wife is about to leave them. The Winchester used to keep records. They promised that your performance would be completely confidential, but somehow your results always got out. And you knew when they did. After a particularly bad couple of months a few years ago, where I had lost something like ten grand, people stopped looking at me when they said hi. Sometimes the club is worse than high school.

At the game's peak in the late 1990s, there must have been about twenty or thirty underground card houses in the five boroughs. And that number doesn't include the ten or so blackjack/blow job joints (they are exactly what they sound like) I knew of. No matter where you were in the city—Staten Island, Yankee Stadium, East New York, Flushing, the Village—you were never more than twenty minutes from a joint.

Depending on how safe you wanted to feel, you really could choose to play at any one of the card houses. There were tiny gypsy joints in the west Forties, Russian clubs out in Astoria, Queens, Chinese and Italian places on Mott Street. Almost every legitimate social organization or backgammon or chess club had a poker game running in the back room. Any of them would do if you were interested in a small-stakes game. But if you were looking for a big game, and the slightest peace of mind that you were not about to have a gun shoved down your throat, then there were really only two places in the city to choose from: the Winchester in the financial district and the Heart Club on Manhattan's West Side.

Games were usually offered from four in the afternoon until sunup. They ranged from a $1–$5 rotation (a game with alternating rounds of stud, Omaha, and Hold'em) to the $10,000 no-limit game at the Winchester. Even though the two clubs were in direct competition with one another, they shared many of the same customers. It was pretty common for a player to run well in the pot-limit game at the Heart and then slide over to the Winchester later that night for a game of $75–$150 rotation .

The Heart Club was run by two middle-aged Irish brothers, William and Joseph. Their club was on the second floor of a two-story Chelsea building and would have dispelled even the slightest suspicion of glamour in poker. Not that either of the brothers were rude or tough or unpleasant—they were actually both very decent people. It was just that the Heart Club was seedy. You entered through a wire gate, the stairwell reeked of rotting, damp animal fur, and the neighborhood strongly resembled a demilitarized zone. Once you got upstairs, there were no windows, the carpet was so incredibly filthy that the stains looked almost like a pattern, and the whole thing was like one giant smoking section. Yet if you were not the first to arrive, it was almost impossible to get a seat at one of the eight tables.

Unlike the owners of the Winchester, who tried to break as few laws as possible while running their club, the McCoy brothers' only concern was keeping their joint packed at all times. They did anything imaginable to promote the club. They ran tournaments. They offered a bad-beat jackpot; the dealers would chop $1 out of every hand that was played, which went into a pool that built until somebody lost a hand with aces full of jacks, full house, or better. When that happened, 50 percent of the jackpot went to the loser, 25 percent to the winner, and the rest got split up between everybody else seated at a table at that time. When the bad-beat jackpot got to $20,000, there wasn't an open seat in the place for months.

Those promotional gimmicks eventually caused a huge problem. The Winchester survived as long as it did because it was technically a private club that charged an annual fee for membership. There were no dealers at the tables and collection boxes full of chips. That way they were able to deny some knowledge of what was going on in the club. That provided a little bit of legal wiggle room for the owners as they tried to justify the activities that were going on there. The Heart Club's very public offering of poker to the community allowed for no such ambiguity. There was no other way to see the activities going on at the Heart Club than as violations of every antigambling law in New York City. The bad-beat jackpot resembled a private lottery, which in itself is a criminal offense.

The police, who once were willing to ignore the activities at the Winchester, and the district attorney, who was reluctant to prosecute the owners because of the ambiguity in the law relating to games of skill, now had no choice but to recognize the activities going on right under their noses. Early in the year 2000 the police department started to take a keen interest in both poker clubs. They were raided and shut down a number of times but continued to reopen in the hopes that the city was just making a token effort and had no real intention of pursuing prosecution. That turned out to be true to some extent. The district attorney didn't prosecute the owners criminally, but the corporation counsel, which is the civil arm of the district attorney's office, did pursue the club owners for multiple violations of city codes. Facing huge fines and also the threat of criminal prosecution, everybody shut down in August 2000. For about two months it was almost impossible to find a game of poker in New York City.

That drought ended as many of the old employees of the Heart and Winchester clubs started opening smaller clubs of their own. Sandy M. was one such entrepreneur. Having worked in Los Angeles card rooms for fifteen years, Sandy moved east when he heard that all the New York card clubs had gone out of business.

"It certainly seemed like a perfect time to go into business for myself," said Sandy.

> L.A. is a poker player's heaven. But between Hollywood Park, the Bicycle Club, Commerce, and Larry Flynt's Hustler Casino, there's too much competition out there. When everybody is starting over in a town like New York or Boston, that's the time to get in. Seeing how the guys who just got shut down were treated by the city, it looked like they weren't really trying to put guys away, so if you have a clean record like I do, you open your

club, run it till you get too much heat, take your slap on the wrist, and then walk away. Everybody thinks the key to running a place in New York is connections—knowing enough cardplayers to keep your club packed, and knowing people on both sides of the law who will help you keep the club running. That kind of stuff helps, but it's not everything. The key to running a great club is running it well. A perfect example is the Hollywood Park Casino in Los Angeles.

But that's a little bit different, because it isn't hard to run a club in a town where you're not doing anything wrong. If the law says it's okay, you just run the room like a casino in Vegas or A.C. does. There are certain states that don't allow regular gambling. No cards, dice, nothing like that. But poker is okay. For some reason, it's not thought of as gambling like other games. The law sometimes calls it a game of skill. You can't open a dice table in L.A., but poker's okay.

So you run those houses just like any other business. You try to keep your customers happy and make sure nobody, especially your own people, is ripping you off. In a place like L.A., the trick there is to do anything you can to keep the players happy. You give them free stuff to make them feel important. I used to walk around the floor at HP with a packet of free parking coupons. I'd see some guy who looks sort of familiar, like he's been around some, so I go up, ask his name, introduce myself, and then tell him how much we appreciate his business. But here's the good part. We appreciate his business so much that I want to give him this VIP, priority, super-duper first class free parking pass, good for the whole month. The guy goes nuts like he's just been knighted or asked to be part of a crew or something. Now, I know it's nice to get a nod every once in a while, but come on, parking is free at HP. So instead of parking 100 feet away in the lot, this guy gets to drive up to the front and valet for free. But he's still got to tip the guy, right. And then his car gets taken to the spot he would have parked in anyway. So think about it. The valet makes his money, this guy's car is in the same spot it would have been anyway, yet he feels like a big shot. Who can figure these people out? I kept an eye on that guy. He came once a week like clockwork, but after I gave him the parking pass, he doubled up for the entire month. That's the kind of ridiculous thing you got to do.

One way the clubs try to separate themselves from one another is non-gambling-related services that they provide. The Hollywood Park Casino happens to have the best Asian food in L.A. "The food's key," Sandy continued.

You make it so that these guys never want to leave their seat. That's real important because the only way the house makes money is collect a table fee, you know, the chop. You make it so they got a reason to stay seated. The more time they sit in your place and pay the chop, the more stuff you give them. You also got to remember that these are people that are sitting in one place for hours. So you need to be able to feed them good food that don't cost too much. Bring them the food on carts so they don't have to miss a hand. Our menu at HP was so big that you could order pancakes, pad thai, fries with gravy and the Dover sole. You've never seen anything like it. Desserts, after-dinner drinks. Really, the only thing better than what we had was Vegas. The longer they sit there, the more money the house chops. Get some people to walk around and offer massages. But if poker ain't legal in your town, now that's a totally different thing.

"There are three keys to running a private club," said Sandy's partner, John K., who used to manage one of Boston's biggest card rooms.

First, and I better read this in your book, we always operated thinking that the services we provided were completely legal in the Commonwealth of Massachusetts. We ran a private club. We charged a membership fee. And most importantly, we allowed our members to participate in games of skill on which we, as the club, had no vested interest in the outcome. Yes, some money changed hands between some people, but that happens at bridge clubs, country clubs, golf courses. The next thing you want to do is make sure that all the players are comfortable. I don't mean physically, you got to get them comfortable in their heads. You got make it so they can walk into your club with $3,000 in cash in their pockets and they feel safe. The guys at the Winchester used to have these necklaces that were panic buttons that if they pressed it, an alarm would go straight to the local police precinct. That's what they used to tell you anyway, who knows if that was true. But it sure did make the players there feel a whole lot more comfortable.

The last essential component to running a private club is banking. You have to have a credit line, a banker who has confidence in you. That's because you're going to end up being a bank of sorts yourself. Only difference is that your clients are going to be the worst degenerates of New York. Theoretically, every penny that you pay out has been paid in because everybody's buying chips. But that doesn't always happen, because often the people playing at your club are broke most of the time. So part of the appeal of playing at your place is that you will lend them money. And when they lose, you have to be patient with a pay schedule, or they might never come back again. The one thing you have in your benefit is that you let them play on credit. Nobody ever disappears for good.

The last essential component of a card club is the shill. A shill is a player who is supported by the house, but plays in the games as an individual. Often a game that is supposed to start at eight o'clock will not have enough players to start until ten. This is bad for business.

"You want your games to be like clockwork," said Sandy. "You want people to know that on a certain date, at a certain time, they are guaranteed to get their poker fix at your club." That's where the shill comes in. They hang around the club and dip into any game that is shorthanded.

The quality of the club can often be determined by the quality of the shill. At the unsavory joints, the house players are often told to make as much money as possible. They are cutthroat and sleazy and awful to play with. The house depends on their winnings as part of its income. At the more reputable clubs the shills are there just to fill space. They are instructed to play as conservatively as possible. They are just there to keep the games going. That's it.

One of the great misconceptions about poker is that the house employees are good players. Most of the time they're not. Sure, a shill plays a lot of poker, they see lots of hands a year, but if they were really any good, they wouldn't be making the equivalent of $10 an hour playing a $5-10 Omaha game at four o'clock on Tuesday. The shill is to a real poker player what the warm-up rider is to a jockey. The people you should watch out for at the card club are the owners. They do play with the house's money, and are often sitting on lower-stakes games than they are used to. "The owners take your money to try and earn your respect," said Sandy. "They think that will be part of the reason you'll come back to their club."

A few hours after conducting the interview with Sandy at his club, I lost about $1,500 to him in a game of pot-limit Texas Hold'em. I haven't been back to his club since.

I CALL

I stayed up all night playing poker with tarot cards. I got a full house and four people died.

—STEVEN WRIGHT,
comedian

The few seconds between calling the final bet and actually getting to see your opponent's cards are genuine hell. It's this nauseating abyss of a moment, composed of nothing but second-guessing yourself and insecurity about your own abilities. Every action that took place during that hand always comes back to me. Every bet and raise, every stutter and twitch, gets scrutinized in my head. Maybe I'm a pessimist. Maybe I've just never become as good a cardplayer as I hoped to. But there is often a loathing that fills me while I wait for those two miserable words—*I call*—to drift across the table; a loathing for everything that I've done in my life that led me to that moment of waiting.

It's the passivity inherent in calling that bothers me most.

Great players rarely just match a bet. In fact, Doyle Brunson once said that you should never simply call. You either raise or fold. In his mind, those are the only two options. To be a great cardplayer, you must be the aggressor. If you're just calling, then you're probably losing. And if you're losing, you shouldn't be in the game. That's why drawing hands in poker can be the death of a player. If the guy with the made hand is any good, he's going to make you pay through the nose to chase him down. And remember what happens to chasers . . . husbands get caught, dogs get run over, and cardplayers, they go broke.

That's what made my play against Joey Millman so painful. In the hand I described in the introduction, the turn card was the 5 of diamonds, making the board look like: 6♥ 7♣ K♣ 5♦ . Combine that with my 8♣ 9♣ pocket cards and that giving me a 9-high straight, the nuts. Clearly I was leading at that point. But after the river was dealt, the J♣ , and Joey tapped into me, it looked like I let somebody chase me down. My mistake was that I didn't make him pay to catch up to me.

Even after I called him, I had no idea what Joey's cards were. Dissecting his play is useless. Joey's too good to be predictable. I've seen him raise $400 with a pair of aces and the next hand do the same thing with a suited 6-7. When I called his $2,000 raise with my flush, I did so because if I ended up losing that hand to a higher flush than mine, I wanted to go home. I couldn't have stayed at that table after watching him collect the chips.

It wasn't the simple fact of losing that would send me packing. I've probably lost well over 200,000 poker hands in my life. I'm pretty used to it. And it wasn't the amount of money either. I've parted with more in one hand plenty of times. I once dropped $9,410 in one pot, had enough composure to buy in for another grand, and won back $4,200 by the end of the night. Now, what bothered me most was that I had played so amateurishly. For the first time in my life I thought that maybe, just maybe, I had stopped getting better at poker. That maybe I was at the end of my learning curve, and this incarnation of insecurities and self-doubt was the best that I'd ever be.

The trick to becoming a decent poker player is to set high starting standards. You never call the first bet unless you've got the goods. Do that, and you'll start to improve. To go from decent to profitable, all you have to do is learn to play the game: maximize winnings and minimize losses. But to become great, like Joey Millman, you have to be able to read people. That's what puts you over the top. I can only read *some* people.

My friend Eric Scoleri is always blown away by my ability to put him on a hand. After the game he walks up and asks how I knew what he was holding. It's really not that hard. When he gets a good card, his eyes open wide like a kid being handed a lollipop. When he gets a bad card, he flinches like he just stepped on a tack.

Picking that up doesn't make me the Amazing Kreskin. Eric, I got. But when I'm playing with great players, my reads are often completely wrong.

It hurt to come to that conclusion. It was like I let myself down. I didn't mind making mistakes when I was nineteen. When you're the youngest person at the table, you chalk the error up to a learning experience. You comfort yourself by saying that you'll be better than everybody at the table by the time you get to be their age. So you keep playing. But now that I'm the average age, I'm no longer the prodigy just about to blossom. Waiting for Joe to show his cards, I realized that I never took that final step to becoming great.

Too often I lose money I shouldn't have. So why do I still play the game? Was I just hanging on because I was too stubborn to quit? At my cousin's engagement party a few years ago, my father was asked by an old family friend what I was doing with my time. I had just walked into the party but was within earshot of their conversation. At that time I was an associate editor at *The Paris Review* literary magazine. My father (a doctor) loved it when I was studying to be a physicist, loved to say that his son was studying to be a rocket scientist. I guess my desire to become a writer was a disappointment to him. So my father answered the question, "Andy, well, he's a failed astrophysicist." No mention of my employment at one of the most respected literary magazines in the world. No mention of any of the articles I had published. It was like he couldn't let go of what he hoped I would be. Maybe I was doing the same thing. Maybe that's what I had become: a failed poker player, too caught up in what I wanted to be to realize that I had to move on. Was that it? Was I just hanging on?

I definitely know why I started to play the game. My first hand of poker was played on a lake in the Adirondack Mountains. I was eight. Back in those pre–satellite TV/Internet days, summer on upper St. Regis Lake was real family time, swimming and sailing and running around—the days up there were great for a city kid like me. But the nights were awful. My poor mother would try anything to keep my brother and me—two psychotically hyper children—occupied as best she could. One night she suggested a game of poker, played with mini-marshmallows as chips. The game has never meant so much.

As one of the great insomniacs ever to live—and afraid of the dark, not to mention snakes, bears, fish, flying, flying fish, basically everything about being in the Adirondack Mountains—I'd try to keep my family up all night playing poker. I'd beg and plead to keep the games going as long as possible. That was my initial motivation for playing back in the mid-1970s: pure desperation.

High school was different. I had evolved into what most of my teachers considered the class screwup. It wasn't my fault. I just started out ninth grade with what I consider to be the most dangerous emotional composition for a high school environment: I was fairly unremarkable in almost every way. I was a good athlete, but not outstanding. I was actually a very sub-par student due to a bad case of dyslexia. I was small. My one outstanding trait was my desire to do anything to be different. And that, in the mid-1980s, led me to wear a lot of tight black jeans, double-pierce my left ear, and employ an amount of mousse on my hair that defied logic. My best friend Steve and I wore eyeliner (sorry for outing you, buddy). Part of being different at that time was gambling. I liked the negative reputation that being known as a poker player conjured. At that time I played to be unique, to be individual. Most of all, I played to be bad.

By the time I hit college, my intellectual personality began to take form. My years of struggling with the English language (any language, really) in high school led me to a desire to pursue an academic career oriented in mathematics. That was an interesting time in my self-awareness. I was always a good math student in high school, but never amazing. I had more interest in math because I was such a terrible student in other courses. But in college, particularly at Vassar where there were no math or science requirements, anybody who studied math—even somebody like me who was pretty average—was considered a math whiz. Even though I wasn't one, I liked being thought of as a genius. That's why I chose to double-major in physics and astronomy.

It was at that point that I realized poker was a mathematically based game. I began to incorporate my studies into poker and found that I was better than the guys I was playing with. Our game in college was pretty low stakes. If my friend Mike lost more than $100, he'd have to pay people back by filling up their cars using his parents' Mobil credit card. That card game was the first time I ever experienced the joy of being good at anything. And I liked it.

When you are the best player at the poker table, people give you respect. They ask you questions and sincerely think about your responses. I had never been the best at anything, anywhere. So I played in college to stroke my ego and to show off.

I began to play seriously when I attended grad school in Middletown, Connecticut, in 1992. I was studying physics and astronomy at Wesleyan University. At that time, Connecticut was in the throes of a miserable recession. In addition, there were only a handful of grad students at this small, cliquey university. It's no wonder I needed a distraction. My closest friend was a visiting professor who taught my theoretical mathematics class. One night he came by my apartment and asked me if I wanted to go with him to the Foxwoods Casino. I had never felt so at home any place in my whole life. If I ever was a gambling addict, that year was it. I played poker to escape from school and mostly to forget that my mother had just passed away. I played because it was a fantastic way to lose myself.

Even though my time at the Foxwoods Casino was the reason that I basically failed out of graduate school (I dropped out before they threw me out), I left Wesleyan feeling that it was time well spent. I had, after all, learned how to count outs and read basic tells, and most importantly, I had mastered the principle of pot odds.

When I moved back to New York, I found it a very different place than when I had left. All of my friends who encouraged me to leave school so they could have somebody to get drunk with did the unthinkable; they got jobs. I played poker back then because I had nothing else to do with my days. I couldn't really find a job that fit my idiosyncratic ideal of working. So I started playing in Atlantic City and in underground clubs to pass the time. At a time in life when people defined themselves by occupation first and foremost, poker served as my identity. There was something sexy about playing in those poker games, something romantic about this group of people who tried to make a living in such an unorthodox manner. For a short period in the mid-1990s, I actually considered playing poker professionally for the rest of my life. Luckily, I didn't have the bankroll to lose more than I won as I learned the finer points of the game, and eventually I sold out and got a job. I didn't play poker once in 1995.

I tried my hand at a number of different jobs before landing the gig at *The Paris Review.* I loved it there. The emotional and monetary security I derived from gainful employment allowed me to go back to playing poker regularly without the burden of having to win. That's when I started to play beautifully. For the first time since college and the late 1980s, I could really see the improvement in my play. I really thought that I was going to end up being one of the greats.

The definitive moment in my poker playing career took place in 1997, when a gaming magazine called *Chance* asked me to write about playing poker in a casino. That article caught the attention of a writer at *Esquire* named Ken Kurson. Ken called me one day and asked if I'd take him to Atlantic City next time I went down. I escorted Ken to the Taj poker room and showed him the ropes. I let him look over my shoulder in a $15–$30 Hold'em game. In one of my first hands, I was dealt the king and queen of spades. The flop had two spades in it. There were about five other players in the hand, and the betting was very lively. The turn card was the ace of spades, giving me the nuts. When the card hit the table, Ken clapped his hands, actually said, "Woo-hoo!" and then slapped my back. Of course, after I bet, everybody folded. I leaned over to Ken and said, "You can't do that. You're giving my cards away to the rest of the table."

Ken thought for a second. "Of course, you're right," he said. "You know what, you should write a book about this."

By the time I wrote this book, I had decided that I wasn't ever going to be good enough to play poker professionally. I'd never get to be one of the big boys. The book, however, made all of the time I wasted playing poker, all the bad beats I'd taken, seem worthwhile. But the question still stood, what the hell was I doing, sitting across from Joey Millman with $3,000 at stake?

Joey begins to turn his cards over. He's moving in slow motion. I stare at the cards on the board: 6♥ 7♣ K♣ 5♦ J♣. Even though I'm still nauseous, I don't think I'm going to throw up anymore because I know it's almost over. Thank God, it's almost over. Maybe another second and my heart will slow down, the sweat will dry, and I can limp home.

Joey's smile disappears. He's about to speak. Two pair or flush. Two pair or flush. I still have no idea what his cards are. His upper teeth hit his lower lip. That's certainly not how you look when you're about to make a "t" sound. No, it's definitely an "f."

"F . . . FLUSH!" Joey says almost apologetically.

Shit. I'm such a loser. Why do I do this to myself? I'm about to toss my cards into the muck when I remember that I've got a flush too. Joey's a tough guy. If he had the ace of clubs, he'd certainly have taken great pleasure in announcing that he had the best hand. He would have said "nuts," not flush. He flips his cards over and reaches for the chips.

He played the 5♣ 4♣. He flopped a flush draw and an open-ended straight draw. Turned a pair. And rivered the flush. After the turn, the great Joey Millman was drawing dead to little old me. He had absolutely zero outs.

If you take too long to announce your winning hand, it's called "slow rolling." It's considered very rude. I never do it. Well, I did once. I just wanted to let Joey's hands touch the chips before I told him that I had a higher flush. So I waited. That moment couldn't have been long enough.

"No good, Joey," I said, laying down my cards.

Watching him watch me stack his chips, that's when I realized why I still play the game. Because I love it. Because Hold'em is the perfect game. And I'm an excellent poker player.

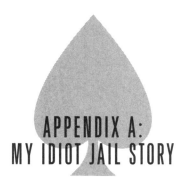

APPENDIX A:
MY IDIOT JAIL STORY

It was a beautiful January day in 1992, and I was driving back to New York from Washington, D.C. There was a card game taking place in my apartment, and I was eager to get to it. Back when I was twenty-three, I was reckless. I thought very little about the impact my actions had on others. There is perhaps no better example of that than the way I drove. It was too fast, too careless, and if you ignore the fact that I wore eyeliner in high school, it is the thing that I am most embarrassed of.

That said, I was driving home from D.C. absurdly fast in a car I had bought for $6,000 earlier that year. It was the most beat-up 1972 Porsche 911T ever. The car was, and still is, Kermit the Frog green with California plates, and though it looks kind of shabby, it rides unbelievably well. That day the weather was inexplicably temperate for early January, something like 50 degrees. I, of course, had the top off, the music blaring, I was wearing my sunglasses and smoking like seven cigarettes at a time.

I was driving very quickly, and for the entire span of Baltimore County, I don't think I looked in my rearview mirror once. After some time of genuinely oblivious driving joy, I became aware of a police helicopter hovering over me. It was at that point I decided to check the condition of the world behind me. In my rearview mirror, I noted a phalanx of police cars about a mile or two in the distance. I looked down at my speedometer, which read 125 m.p.h. (the ticket I was issued said 135). I knew there was no way to get out of this one. I was definitely getting a ticket. I pulled my car to the shoulder and waited for the cops. When the first officer reached my window, I had my license and registration in my hand, ready to hand it over. Instead, I was torn from my seat and cuffed on the hood of my car within seconds.

The magical saving grace of the story is that, in the process of cuffing me, the officer broke my nose, causing me to bleed all over my very '80s Armani suit. He then read me my rights and took me to his car, where he informed me of what I was being charged with. Among the seventeen moving violations and four misdemeanors he listed was a charge of evading police, which I did not think I was guilty of. So I protested.

"Come on," the cop said, "no doubt you were evading."

"Sir," I replied to the angry, macho southern officer, "if I was really trying to evade, I think my car will do like 150, there's no way you would have caught me."

That was the start of an unbelievable series of hideous blunders. The cop pulled out his official NASCAR racing license and said, "Don't get in a pissing contest with me boy, 'cause I'll piss all over you. No way was a little drug-dealing California shit like you gonna outrun me." On my way to jail I tried desperately to convince him that I was not questioning his driving skills or his virility by my comment, but he was sticking to his figurative (at this point) guns.

I was placed in a holding cell, where I waited an hour before being taken to the commissioner of bail. There, alone with my thoughts, I came to understand the essence of necessity. I desperately contemplated my immediate future. In the cruiser, I had asked the cop if I was being taken to prison. He said no, that I was being taken to jail first, then the commissioner would decide if I was to stay in jail or go to prison.

"What's the difference?" I asked.

"Big one for a kid like you. In jail you may get fucked. In prison there's no doubt you will."

Boy, did my priorities change fast as I pictured a communal shower with hardcore convicts. I no longer wanted to make my card game, or go home, I just didn't want to go to prison. My broken nose felt better already. They could even give me a black eye or a couple of broken ribs. I've lost so many fights in my life I can't even remember them all. Over and over again in my head I kept saying, Please send me to jail, please send me to jail.

After about an hour the cop took me to see the commissioner. Her job was to determine whether or not I presented a risk of flight. If I did, she'd be the one who set my bail in the absence of a judge (it was a Sunday night). It is important to remember that I-95 (Miami to New York) is a well-traveled drug courier route, and I was in an M&M green Porsche with California plates wearing a suit that Don Johnson might have worn in *Miami Vice*.

Holding my license, the commissioner asked me a few simple questions.

"Is your real name Andy Bellin?"

"Well, not really," I said. "My real name is Andrey, but I go by Andy or Andrew."*

I watched her write, in big capital letters, "MANY ALIASES."

Then she asked, "Is this your current address?"

My license still had my Vassar address in Poughkeepsie, New York, on it. "No," I explained, "I just moved up from there to Middletown, Connecticut."

*Please see appendix B.

"What's the address there?"

"It's a dorm."

"The street address?" she wanted to know. And I, of course, had no idea.

She printed "NO FIXED ADDRESS" under MANY ALIASES.

"And what do you do for a living, Mr. Bellin?"

Now that was an excellent question. "I'm a grad student."

"But how do you make your living?"

The answer, "My mother died and left me a bit of money," sounded pretty bad. "I play poker and bartend" didn't sound too sexy either.

"I get paid to do research around the observatory. And I'm on a tuition waiver."

"How much do you make?"

"About seventy dollars a week."

"How much is that car worth, Mr. Bellin?

"I paid six thousand dollars for it."

"And you make seventy dollars a week? Interesting. Bail set at ten thousand dollars. Take him to Baltimore County Correctional."

"Is that jail or prison?" I wanted to know.

After a bit of useless begging and pleading, I was escorted to jail.

Before I was processed, I was thrown into another holding cell with an individual who was just starting a three-year term for manslaughter. He proceeded to steal everything on my person. My watch, earring, money, everything. In his defense, he didn't really "steal" anything, per se. He just politely asked for it. And I was more than happy to give it up.

I remained in Baltimore County Correctional for about forty hours until I made bail. In an agreement with the district attorney, I promised not to bring a police brutality suit against the police for my broken nose, and they dropped every charge but a $305 fine for reckless driving. I didn't even get the speeding ticket. Nor did I have to take a shower with the boys.

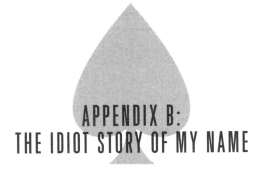

APPENDIX B:
THE IDIOT STORY OF MY NAME

Upon my birth, it was my mother's intention to call me Andrea Della Croce Bellin. Andrea, in Italy, is a very popular, maybe even a macho, name. I think it translates to "courage." That's Italy. In America, Andrea is a girl's name, and my father had no intention of raising a boy named Sue. So on the way to hand in the birth certificate, he thought to champion his son's masculinity by erasing the last "a" from Andrea, and changing it to the Russian Andrei. Now that's a goddamned MAN'S name. It was a touching gesture, except for the fact that my father thought Andrei was spelled with a "y," not an "i." So the name on my birth certificate reads Andrey Della Croce Bellin. Though there are a few other people named Andrey on the planet, seeing my name in print always reminds me of the importance of proofreading.

I have gone through my whole life being called Andrea (both pronunciations), Andrew (most people think the "y" is a typo), and André. My first-grade teacher was so confused that she took to calling me Andy. Bless that woman.

APPENDIX C:
THE POKER LEXICON

Ace high: A poker hand with no pair where the highest card is an ace.

Aces up: Two pair, aces being one of them.

Action: What's going on at the table. Also a measure of how lively a poker game is.

All-in: When all your chips are in play. You got nothing left on the table to bet.

Ante: Money put into the pot at the start of the game.

Backer: A person who finances a poker player.

Bad beat: When a huge hand is beaten by an underdog with an improbable draw.

Bicycle or wheel: A five-high straight.

Blinds: Blind or mandatory bets that initiate a game.

Broadway: An ace-high straight.

Checks: Chips.

Chop, rake, vig, or vigorish: The amount charged by the house for play.

Coffeehousing or Hollywood: Poker play that is augmented by lots of talk or dramatics.

Dead Man's Hand: Two pair, aces and 8s. This term became part of the poker vernacular August 2, 1876, when a cowhand named Jack McCall walked into Carl Mann's Saloon Number 10 in Deadwood, Dakota Territory, and shot the legendary Wild Bill Hickok in the back of the head. Hickok slumped over dead, still holding his poker hand of two pairs—aces and 8s—which has been known as Dead Man's Hand ever since.

Double belly-buster: A collection of five cards where two ranks of cards can complete a straight. Example: A player holds a 7-9-10-J-K. Either a queen or an 8 will complete a straight.

Drawing dead: When a player has no chance to win even though they are still drawing cards.

Flop: The first three up cards in Texas Hold'em or Omaha.

Free roll: When a player is tied with another, but has a draw to a higher hand that the other doesn't. Example: In Texas Hold'em, both players have played a suited Q-J as their hole cards, one in spades, the other in hearts. The flop comes: Q of diamonds, 5 of spades, 9 of spades. Both have a pair of queens with a jack kicker, but the player with the Q-J of spades is free-rolling on the flush draw.

Gut shot or belly-buster: An inside straight draw. Example: You hold a 5-6-8-9. Your draw to a 7 is a gut shot.

Muck: The pile of discards.

The nuts: When you have the highest possible hand on the table. Example: In Texas Hold'em, the board is 2-5-7-9-A with no three of one suit (thus ruling out a flush). A player would have the nuts if they held a 6-8, making a 9-high straight.

Outs: Any cards that, if drawn, will give you the winning hand.

Put: Assuming someone's hand. If you think they have a pair of aces, then you *put* them on aces.

Quads: Four of a kind.

Rabbit hunting: Looking through the discards or undealt part of the deck. Usually rabbit hunting is the precursor to setting up a deck.

River: The last card dealt in a game.

Rock: A player who takes very few chances.

Rollers, roll-ups, or **rolled-up**: In seven-card stud, when your first three cards are all of the same rank.

Set: Three of a kind made while holding a pocket pair. As opposed to "trips," which is also three of a kind, but when the pair is on the board, not in your hand.

Six tits: Three queens.

Splash: When a player throws his chips into the pot before anybody can confirm that it is the right amount of money.

Steel wheel: A five-high straight flush.

Tap: To bet all your chips; to go all-in.

Tell: A player's mannerism that gives away his hand.

Tilt: When a player get knocked off his game and starts to play badly. This usually follows a bad beat.

Turn: The fourth up card in Texas Hold'em or Omaha.

Texas Hold'em Starting Hands:

A-A: American Airlines, Pocket Rockets, or Sticks.

A-K: Big Slick.

A-J: Ajax.

A-10: Bookends or a Johnny Moss.

A-3: Baskin-Robbins (as in 31 flavors).

K-K: Cowboys or Ace Magnets.

K-Q: The Marriage (the Divorce, if it doesn't hold up).

K-J: Kojak.

K-9: The dog; canine.

Q-Q: Dames. Broads. Ladies. Four tits. Siegfried & Roy.

Q-J: Oedipus Rex or Maverick.

Q-10: Quint.

Q-7: Computer hand.

Q-3: A San Francisco Busboy . . . a queen with trey.

J-5: Motown.

10-4: Broderick Crawford. Comes from his television show *Highway Patrol* where he used to say "ten, four," all the time.

10-2. The Doyle Brunson. He won the World Series of Poker twice holding these pocket cards.

9-8: Oldsmobile.

8-8: Little Oldsmobile.

7-6: Union Oil.

5-10: Woolworth. Five and dime.

5-7: Heinz.

4-5: Jesse James. He was rumored to have been shot with a .45 caliber gun.

3-9: Jack Benny. For years he claimed to be thirty-nine years old.

3-8: Raquel Welch. You do the math.

3-3: Crabs.

BIBLIOGRAPHY

The chart on page 31 is taken from page 204 of *Winner's Guide to Texas Hold'em Poker*, by Ken Warren.

The information about the origins of the theory of probability came from a calculus textbook by Tom Apostol.

The statistical information used in the chapter "Probability, Statistics and Religion" came from *Probability: An Introduction* by Samuel Goldberg; *A History of Mathematics*, by Victor J. Katz; and through an e-mail correspondence with the professors mentioned.

The roulette information on page 50 was taken from *Chance Rules: An Informal Guide to Probability, Risk, and Statistics*, by Brian S. Everitt.

The chart on page 48 is taken from page 20 of *Winner's Guide to Texas Hold'em Poker*, by Ken Warren.

Almost all of the Benny Binion information came from *The Players: The Men Who Made Las Vegas*, edited by Jack Sheehan.

I used A. Alvarez's book *The Biggest Game in Town* as a source for the origins of the World Series of Poker.

The John von Neumann information contained within the "Bluffing" chapter came from *A Beautiful Mind*, by Sylvia Nasar, and *Theory of Games and Economic Behavior,* by John von Neumann and Oskar Morgenstern.

The story of Colonel Abel Streight on page 78 came from the book *Nathan Bedford Forrest,* by Jack Hurst.

The Muhammad Ali information presented on page 81 came from three sources: *King of the World,* by David Remnick; *Muhammad Ali: The People's Champ,* edited by Elliot J. Gorn; and the *New York Times* article "Ali Regains Title, Flooring Foreman," written by Dave Anderson.

The Harry Truman anecdote came from *Truman,* by David McCullough; and David Spanier's *Total Poker.*

The Gamblers Anonymous twenty questions came from their website.

The chart on page 122 is taken from page 195 of *Winner's Guide to Texas Hold'em Poker,* by Ken Warren.

The information about the origins of poker came from Alan Dowling's *The Great American Pastime* and David Spanier's *Total Poker.*

Some of the information in the chapter "Tells" came from the video *Mike Caro's Pro Poker Tells.*

The Poker Tom Story came from the Time, Life book *Gamblers of the Old West.*

Most of the technical cheating information came from *Gambling Scams,* by Darwin Ortiz.

Some information in the chapter "Memory" came from *Your Memory: How It Works and How to Improve It,* by Kenneth L. Higbee, Ph.D.